Searching for Faith

Searching for Faith
A Skeptic's Journey

W. Ross Winterowd

Parlor Press
West Lafayette, Indiana
www.parlorpress.com

Parlor Press LLC, West Lafayette, Indiana 47906

© 2004 by Parlor Press
All rights reserved.
Printed in the United States of America

ISBN 1-932559-30-2 (Paperback); ISBN 1-932559-31-0 (Cloth);
ISBN 1-932559-32-9 (Adobe eBook); ISBN 1-932559-33-7 (TK3)

We gratefully acknowledge permission to reprint from the following works:

"Cy Est Pourtraicte, Madame Ste. Ursule, et Les Unze Mille Vierges" and "The Emperor of Ice Cream." From *The Collected Poems of Wallace Stevens* by Wallace Stevens, copyright 1954 by Wallace Stevens and renewed 1982 by Holly Stevens. Used by permission of Alfred A. Knopf, a division of Random House, Inc.

From *A Rhetoric of Motives* by Kenneth Burke. © 1969 by Kenneth Burke. Published by the University of California Press.

Cover photograph: "Wheeler Peak at Sunrise," Great Basin National Park, Nevada. Copyright (c) 1999 by Don Baccus.

SAN: 254-8879

Library of Congress Cataloging-in-Publication Data

Winterowd, W. Ross.
  Searching for faith : a skeptic's journey / W. Ross Winterowd.
    p. cm.
  Includes bibliographical references.
  ISBN 1-932559-31-0 (alk. paper) -- ISBN 1-932559-30-2 (pbk. : alk. paper) -- ISBN 1-932559-32-9 (adobe ebook) -- ISBN 1-932559-33-7 (tk3 ebook)
  1. Christianity. 2. Pragmatism. 3. Winterowd, W. Ross. I. Title.

BR124.W56 2004
230--dc22
                                        2004018205

Printed on acid-free paper.

Parlor Press, LLC is an independent publisher of scholarly and trade titles in print and multimedia formats. This book is also available in cloth, as well as in Adobe eBook and Night Kitchen (TK3) formats, from Parlor Press on the WWW at http://www.parlorpress.com. For submission information or to find out about Parlor Press publications, write to Parlor Press, 816 Robinson St., West Lafayette, Indiana, 47906, or e-mail editor@parlorpress.com.

For our grandsons:
>Christopher Ross Winterowd
>Bryce Watson Winterowd
>Braden Graham Winterowd

Contents

Prologue		xi
1	Prelude	3
2	Prayer	21
3	Seeking Faith: Scripture	36
4	Saint Augustine Learns to Read Scripture	59
5	Sin and Guilt	70
6	Augustine's Sin	80
7	The Bible: The Enigmas	86
8	Conceiving God	102
9	God: The Message	115
10	Christianity and Capitalism	137
11	A Pragmatist's Faith	151
Notes		167
Bibliography		171

Prologue

This is not a scholarly book (though underlying it are a massive amount of reading and hundreds of pages of notes and abortive attempts to get my thoughts down). It is also not a confession (though my beliefs and idiosyncrasies are inevitably apparent throughout). In these pages, I explore questions that must trouble anyone who searches for faith: What is the nature and logic of prayer? Why does prayer seem to be a necessity, even for skeptics? How do believers rationalize the apparent contradictions and the obscurities in the Bible? (In the brief fourth chapter, I give an account of how my favorite saint and theologian, Augustine, explained the Bible to himself.) How can a Christian reconcile twenty-first century American capitalism with his or her faith? What "message" do the Old and New Testaments convey?

I conclude this book with a plea for a native creed, completely American, not imported from the church fathers or the fashionable Gallic philosophers, but derived largely from the joyful, amiable, and brilliant works of John Dewey and William James and expressed in the poetry of Walt Whitman and Wallace Stevens.

Dylan Thomas told us,

> Do not go gentle into that good night,
> Old age should burn and rave at close of day;
> Rage, rage against the dying of the light.

As my end nears, I do not rage against the dying of the light; I rage in the glare of horrors that surround me. The air that my grandsons will breathe is becoming more and more polluted, and there is no remedy in a world that is dominated increasingly by corporations, those impersonal nonentities that have stolen the rights with which citizens were endowed by "The Bill of Rights" and the Constitution. My grandsons will choke on the effluence from out-of-control capitalism.

The National Science Foundation tells us that the world is now spending its capital of natural resources rather than living on the interest. In the future (in the lifetimes of my grandsons?), water will be a commodity available abundantly to the wealthy, but the increasing masses of the wretched of the earth will go thirsty, and they will starve, for global warming will compound the ravages brought on by overpopulation and the diminishing ability of the earth to yield its bounty of grains.

Who can be so out of it as to think that nuclear war is *not* a possibility moment by moment? Will my grandsons survive a minor exchange or a major nuclear holocaust? Will humanity?

I now realize that this book on my search for faith ought to consist of two parts: the first, my view of politics and economics, only the second part dealing with the search. For, after all, my terminal condition and my existence in a world gone mad prompted me to read, think, and write. (As for my terminal condition: for a person who spent a good deal of his life abusing his body, I am amazingly healthy. However, the condition of each of us is terminal; it's just that my end is nearer than the ends of many of us.)

What makes life in this horrendous world possible is one aspect of my faith: my hope for the future. I have hope that my grandsons will live in a better world than the one I now inhabit. The revival of interest in the Christian life brings me hope, not, of course, through the rantings, the madness, or the smooth truisms of some popular preachers, but in various church groups, such as the Society of Friends, who commit themselves to social action.

And through Christ's message of love, I have joy in the moment of living.

Alfred North Whitehead's statement about the person and his or her religion is the epigraph for my first chapter, but so meaningful is this thought that I don't hesitate to inscribe it twice in these pages.

> Your character is developed according to your faith. This is the primary religious truth from which no one can escape. Religion is force of belief cleansing the inward parts. For this reason the primary religious virtue is sincerity, a penetrating sincerity.
> (*Religion in the Making*, 15)

In the first chapter, I have attempted, with, I hope, a penetrating sincerity, to tell of the development of my character through my early years. However, this autobiographical narrative is quite different in tone from the rest of the book, for Chapters 2 through 8 background my own experience and foreground the problems of faith. I do think, however, that the first chapter explains my motives and the experiential equipment that I bring to the questions that I ask in this book.

I hope that those who go through these pages will find the book as valuable in the reading as it was to me in the writing.

Finally, I would like to thank editor-publisher David Blakesley for his wise guidance and for his meticulous work on the manuscript. David is a bookperson in the great tradition of Lawrence Ferlinghetti of City Lights and James Laughlin of New Directions.

Searching for Faith
A Skeptic's Journey

1

Prelude

> Your character is developed according to your faith. This is the primary religious truth from which no one can escape. Religion is force of belief cleansing the inward parts. For this reason the primary religious virtue is sincerity, a penetrating sincerity.
>
> —Alfred North Whitehead, *Religion in the Making*

Faith is not rational, in the sense that through a chain of logic I can prove that my beliefs are true. However, it is not irrational to believe in an omniscient, omnipotent deity—though some of the conclusions based on that belief are clearly mad. I think—and I am not alone in this—that the quest for the ultimate, for the faith that there is a power of some kind controlling destiny—a final answer (perhaps never to be found)—is inevitably human. The person who denies that quest, or finds it "irrational," silly, vain, and nugatory does not participate fully in the adventure that is humanity.

It goes without saying that belief in a religion is in large part cultural. A child growing up in a Mormon town in central Utah is quite likely to remain with that faith; a child in an Italian-American family and culture is likely to be a Catholic for life. To understand why a person professes a religion, you must know that person's background.

When I was eight years old, I was baptized into the Church of Jesus Christ of Latter Day Saints. I was then officially a Mormon.

I can relive that day—now more than sixty years ago—as vividly as if it were the present. My maternal grandmother, whom I called Nanny, and my Aunt Lucile, my mother's sister, took me to the Mormon Tabernacle in Salt Lake City. The baptistery, on the west end of the building, in a space created by the tiered platform above it in the main auditorium of the Tabernacle, was the site of a large font, a giant bowl supported by twelve marble oxen. (Or were the oxen brass? Perhaps my memory is not as sharp as I had thought it was.) In a dressing room, I changed from my street clothes into a white robe and came to the font for the rite. The baptist uttered "In the name of the Father and of the Son and of the Holy Ghost, I baptize thee...." And I was immersed.

Marble oxen? Bronze oxen? What I do remember, what I am sure of, is that I thought, as I walked with Nanny and Aunt Lucile from the Temple Grounds in Salt Lake City, "Well, now I won't sin any more." I remember that moment so vividly, and I also remember how tepid it was, how lacking in passion, how void of joy and mystery, how colorless. I had done what Nanny and Aunt Lucile wanted of me. And no longer would I commit the horrendous sins that baptism had washed from my soul.

Tucking me in bed at night, my Nanny would kiss me and say, "Don't play with your Johnnie." So now, washed clean of sin, I would no longer play with my Johnnie. I would no longer let my pals tempt me into pilferage at the five-and-dime. I would no longer (shades of St. Augustine) steal apples from the neighbor's tree.

My mother and father were both skeptics, perhaps atheists; in any case, there was no religion in the home—actually, a series of flats in rundown buildings—I shared with them: no blessings before meals, no bedtime prayers, no Bible readings. I doubt that there was a Bible in the apartment, though my father read aloud from *The First Mortgage*, a doggerel verse summary of the Bible:

> Sometime, and somewhere out in space,
> God felt it was the proper place

> To make a word, as he did claim,
> To bring some honor to his name.

But having his doubts, God consults Truth, Justice, and Mercy. Truth and Justice give stern warnings about their relationship to the Creatures; however

> [Mercy] said, "If man should go astray,
> I'll point to him another way,
> And by the mercy that I give,
> Poor fallen man again may live."

So

> The Lord adopted Mercy's plan,
> And made the world—also the man.
> This is the way the thing was done,
> Without a ray of light or sun;
>
> Away out there alone, above,
> Without a thing to make it of,
> The world was made without a flaw,
> Without a hammer or a saw,
>
> Without a bit of wood or stone,
> Without a bit of flesh or bone,
> Without a board or nail or screw,
> Or anything to nail it to.

This, then, was the only scripture that I knew. Ending with the sacrifice of Jesus on the cross, it wasn't impious:

> Thus in the line, direct from Shem,
> A King was born in Bethlehem;
> Great drops of blood for us he sweat,
> And by his death he paid the debt.

However, Father, I think, read it not for its "message," but for the cleverness of the verse and its making light of final questions.

And that constituted the religion in my home.

But I had another home: with Nanny, who was the dearest person in my life. My parents had their own concerns, and I wasn't really one of them, so they often sent me to stay with Nanny. I came home from school not to Mother and Father's apartment, but to Nanny's; I spent more nights of the week at Nanny's than with my parents. And Nanny was a Mormon convert.

I'm certain that she had never read *The Book of Mormon*, perhaps did not own a copy. She probably read Mormon tracts and the magazine for women, *The Improvement Era*. But what I remember of her professed belief is its superstition. For instance, she told me that a person who tithed would receive tenfold in return, the payoff being money, not spiritual benefits or credit with the Almighty. Though adamant in her belief, Nanny was not a church-goer.

Aunt Lucile, on the other hand, was a true blue Mormon. She had read *The Book of Mormon*, or had read in it; she prayed before meals, and when I stayed with her and Uncle Chick (which was quite often), Aunt Lucile supervised my bedtime prayers. She was a teacher in the Mormon program for children, called simply "Primary," and I accompanied her to her classes.

Aunt Lucile was dear to me, taking me, when I was a preschooler, to Liberty Park for endless rides on the merry-go-round, helping me plant onions and radishes in her backyard, taking me to the S. H. Kress five-and-dime lunch counter for egg salad sandwiches—and we bowed our heads and prayed before we ate.

My aunt's loving goodness to me and my deep love for her did not translate into religious passion. In the rituals with Aunt Lucile, I was obedient, but utterly lacking any sense of joy or awe. In fact, I was largely bored.

Then there was Nanny's sister, great-aunt Aunt Dolly, oxymoronically a Catholic spiritualist, who lived in an old two-story house with my great-grandmother. With the drapes always closed, the house was dark and dank. In the living room, the furniture was midnight blue mohair, the fireplace below the dark wood mantle was outlined with rust brown tiles, and the yellow-dial radio with the two large knobs for tuning and volume stood on spindly legs in one corner. The mahogany wardrobes were massive, for the construction of the house had predated closets. The only bathroom was on the mysterious second floor, the rooms of which were sealed and, so far as I knew, unvisited.

My great aunt and my great grandmother terrified me—or, rather, the house and their doings and their tales made me always apprehensive when I was with them, yet they were so indulgent to me that I often asked my parents to let me visit Aunt Dolly and Meemaw (as I called my great-grandmother). Meemaw, who died when I was perhaps four or five, is only a wisp in my memory, but Aunt Dolly was part of my life and dear to me until she died when I was in my thirties. A spectrally thin woman who, after her mother's death, always dressed in black, Aunt Dolly had a Ouija board, but I was forbidden to touch it; its power (whether benign or malign) was too great for a child to tamper with. She fed me endless pastries, especially chocolate éclairs. She told me tales of Aunt Maud, who would ride up to the house on her charger, leap over the iron picket fence, and tie her horse to the porch railing. By the time I heard this story, Aunt Maud had departed.

When I stayed with Aunt Dolly, I was pampered, indulged—and terrified. The sepulchral house with its spectral, black-clad mistress, its darkness and dankness, and its arcane mysteries intensified the fear of the dark that plagued me in my childhood. The house was the meeting place for sundry spiritualists. I was never allowed to participate in the occult doings that took place in the funereal living room, but I heard stories from my uncle and from my mother about speaking trumpets hovering in the gloom and delivering messages from the beyond. My mother, a homespun positivist, told me of seeing Meemaw and Aunt Dolly raise a heavy oak table by the laying on of hands, and my uncle swears that he has seen ghosts in the house.

The second-floor bathroom was a great problem. The thought of going up to that dark, mysterious realm terrified me, and not wanting to climb the stairs with me, Aunt Dolly solved the problem by telling me to peepee down the register into the furnace in the cellar. Since she covered the stench of pee with incense, the house always smelled of the rank odor of urine fused with the spices of the orient.

My Cousin Ethel, Aunt Dolly's niece, was frequently at the house, and I always knew whether or not she was there when I came in the front door, for Cousin Ethel's body odor was so rank that it permeated the whole place. She was a huge woman. Four hundred pounds? Perhaps. More? Maybe. When she sat on a kitchen chair (in her pink dress with giant blue polka dots) her belly between her spraddled legs sagged almost to the floor. She wore cheap jewelry, rings on every finger, necklaces, earrings. Her unwashed, greasy hair was a mass of bobby pins. And her language, even in my presence, was vile.

Aunt Dolly had a thriving home business, making curtains and drapes for Sears customers and doing chenille letters and insignias for the local high schools and the University of Utah. Her work room, with its sewing and embroider machines, was between the parlor and the kitchen. When business was particularly brisk, Aunt Dolly hired Cousin Ethel to help with the work; thus, Ethel was often at the house when I was there, adding her corpulent fetidness to the eeriness of the place.

On Easter and Christmas Eve, I went to mass with Aunt Dolly. I remember how the splendor of the Cathedral of the Madeleine contrasted with the utilitarian plainness of Aunt Lucile's Mormon ward. The Latin mass, the stained glass windows, the organ peeling forth its anthems, the stations of the cross, the spicy smell from the censer—these were mysterious and beautiful. The Mormon ward always smelled clean, as if every nook and cranny had been scrubbed with strong soap. It was an everyday, utilitarian sort of place. There was no mystery.

Aunt Dolly was convinced that Christ would appear precisely at the stroke of twelve on Christmas Eve, and appear He did. She saw Him year after year and whispered excitedly to me, "There He is. Do you see Him?"

Though my maternal grandfather had died before I was born, I knew my paternal grandfather, a railroad man from Iowa. My earliest memory of him is when he came to Salt Lake City for a two-week visit in the summer. He was a reticent, stern man whom I never did get to know, not even after he retired and moved to Salt Lake City and lived in the same apartment building as my parents.

Grandfather was a church-going Methodist, and I remember the endlessness of the services that he in effect forced me to sit through when he came for his summer vacation. The interminable sermons. The wheezing console organ, with the organist pumping steadily on the treadles. The hard pews. The summer heat and the smell of sweat. The only relief was looking forward to the cool watermelon, to be eaten in Aunt Esther's backyard.

To sum up the religion that I was exposed to before the age of about ten: My mother and father had never professed themselves as atheists and may not have been, but my mother was totally indifferent to religion, and my father was downright hostile to Mormonism. Nanny and Aunt Lucile gave me a tepid experience with the Mormon Church. Aunt Dolly's amalgamation of spiritualism and Catholicism didn't puzzle me at the time, but she didn't want me to tamper with spiritualism, and she (a twice-a-year church goer) did not encourage me to become a Catholic. My grandfather was a solid Protestant who believed that the Catholics were plotting to take over the United States (hence their fortress-like cathedrals), but aside from subjecting me to church services twice during the summer, he had no influence on my beliefs or practices. And such is the religious heritage of my childhood.

In 1946, after my father had obtained work with Consolidated Copper in McGill, Nevada, I entered high school in Ely, thirteen miles from McGill, as a sophomore. McGill was the grimmest and drabbest of company towns. My pals and I used to sing our own version of "Home on the Range":

> Oh, give me a land
> Where you always breathe sand,
> Where the coyotes and jackrabbits play,

> Where always is heard
> A dirty cuss word,
> And the skies they are smoky all day.
> Home, home in McGill,
> To hell with the smelter and mill,
> Where always is heard
> A dirty cuss word,
> And the skies they are smoky all day.

Perhaps the largest group of believing church-goers in McGill were Mormons, and the closest friends of our family were members of this group.

They were a case study in religious tolerance. June and Mike Robb drank their coffee (a Mormon taboo) and had their occasional highball. In fact, on occasion Mike drank quantities of Green Death (i.e., Carlings Red Cap Ale). Evelyn Johnson was a proud teetotaler who told us she had never tasted alcohol, tea, coffee, or tobacco; yet she was an avid gambler, partnering with my father in cutthroat bridge games for stakes that at the time were very large. .

After Consolidated Copper (subsequently Kennecott) fired my father because of his attempt to organize the workers, he gravitated to the saloon and gambling business, but made a large part of his income from freelance card games: bridge, primarily, but also hearts and pinochle. Evelyn and my father won a considerable amount of money in a bridge game with the owner of the Big Four, Ely's brothel.

What I'm getting at is the effect of time and place on religious practice. There were certainly Mormons who obeyed "The Word of Wisdom," the Mormon code for clean living, but even Mormon Bishop Conrad was a sociable part of the strange community, though I think he probably never did go behind the swinging half-doors that separated the ice cream counter from the bar and gambling tables in the McGill Club.

Father McDenough, a whiskey priest straight out of a Graham Greene novel, was a family friend who in the wee hours of the morning, after the saloon had closed, would join my father and mother in our apartment above the J. C. Penney store for liquid refreshments and sandwiches. (My father was not a teetotaler, but he imbibed moderately and infrequently; hence, Father McDenough drank his Old Crow solo, while my father and mother sipped their coffee.)

When I asked my father about the priest's unpriestly conduct, Dad explained that Catholics believe priests hold spiritual powers which are indissoluble. "Once a priest, always a priest," was Dad's summation.

In any case, during my teenage years the believers whom I knew were, to say the least, latitudinarian. No doubt, the Robbs and the Johnsons were sincere believers. I have no reason to doubt Father McDenough's sincerity in his faith. I perceived no contradiction between the creeds these folk subscribed to and their actions; in fact, religion was outside the scope of my life and interests.

Like every other student in public schools and then in state universities, I learned nothing about theology and experienced no religion. In *The Idea of a University*, John Henry Newman had made the point that theology is a branch of knowledge and, hence, should have a place in the curriculum. The separation of church and state is a great American principle, but the exclusion of theology (i.e., knowledge about religion) from public education is lamentable, and lamentably I learned nothing about Christianity, Islam, Buddhism, Hinduism or any of the other religions during my high school and college days. In fact, I knew very little about Mormonism, the religion into which I had been baptized.

And then I married a Mormon from a family of committed believers. Three of my brothers-in-law are or have been bishops. All of my many nieces and nephews and great-nieces and great-nephews go on missions for the Church. The Graham family tree is in the Latter Day Saint orchard.

Norma Graham, I now realize, saved my life; I also realize that I nearly ruined hers. In *Common Prayers*, Harvey Cox chronicles a mixed marriage. He a Christian, his wife a Jew, they have kept their faiths, each enriching the other, but such was not the case during the first two or three decades of our marriage.

I was hostile to religion, particularly Mormonism, pathologically so, but I was and am deeply in love with Norma; I needed her and still need her, and I suppose she needed me; now I know that she needs me. *Wahlverwandtschaften*—elective affinities. *Wahnverwandtschaften*—crazy affinities? Some doggerel verse that pleases both of us: I'm no good, and neither are you. / We're codependent; that's sure true." Let's see if I can explain what was going on in my mind and our marriage.

The Graham home in Fairview, a small town in central Utah, was Mormon through and through. The Lassons, Mother Graham's family, had been pioneers; Grandpa Lasson had walked from Laramie, the terminus of the railroad, to Salt Lake City and thence southward to Sanpete County, the locus of Fairview. The Grahams and the Lassons had never really been out of their home territory. Norma tells of her excitement when her father took her and sister Beulah to Salt Lake City for the annual teachers' institute—the dazzling bright lights, the department stores on Main Street and Third South Street, the traffic, the clanging trolleys and the whishing electric buses, the lunch counter in the Woolworth store, the movie theaters, and, in particular, a woman smoking a cigarette in public.

Mormonism in Fairview was, like Judaism, not only a religion, but a way of life. Young people socialized at the weekly meetings of the Mutual Improvement Association; the MIA Gold and Green Ball was the social event of the year. Funerals were social get-togethers, with potluck banquets provided by the Relief Society, the organization for Mormon women. No coffee or tea, let alone wine.

With eight children, Maitland, my father-in-law, and Marcella, my mother-in-law, had little time for frivolity and no money for luxuries. Marcella made the dresses that the six girls wore; from the garden behind the house Marcella harvested and bottled enough vegetables to last through the winter. Maitland grew the hogs and cattle that provided the family with meat, and Marcella bottled beef and homemade sausage.

Maitland was a schoolteacher and farmer. In the summer he mowed the alfalfa and stacked the hay, cut the grain and took it to the mill to be ground into cracked wheat for breakfasts and flour for the countless loaves of bread that Marcella baked for the family. He milked four or five cows and sold the cream. (I remember bowls of steaming cracked wheat with cream so heavy that I could eat it with a fork; and I remember home-churned butter slathered on a slice of bread hot from the oven.) Mait stretched the Word of Wisdom to accommodate his love of coffee—though I don't think he ever used the word "coffee"; it was always "java." When Norma and I visited the Fairview home, Mait would always ask me, "How about a cup of java?" But the java, with its pungency, was never brewed or drunk in the house; we partook in the milking shed.

It was a home in which prayer was central. (In her later years, as Marcella grew hard of hearing, her bedtime prayers became stentorian, as though God too was becoming deaf.) The Book of Mormon was more important than the Bible, and the president of the Church was a living prophet of God. Our wedding gift from Maitland and Marcella was a "triple combination": the Book of Mormon, Doctrine and Covenants, and Pearl of Great Price[1] all in one volume. Marcella had inscribed on the fly leaf, "May the truths in these pages bring you much happiness and comfort."

As I think about my in-laws, I realize that they were heroic, and my love for them has grown through the years.

However, during the first part of our marriage, I seethed with hostility against my in-laws and writhed with discomfort when I was visiting the Fairview home. I'm tempted to pour forth a confession, *mea culpa*, a purging of my soul if that were possible. My regret for what I did and did not do haunts me. While I was neurotic and paranoid, my mother-in-law and father-in-law were loving and supportive, and, fortunately for me, we ultimately became close friends.

But my purpose here is to delineate the clash of cultures that was a reason for my search for faith. Chaos and orderliness. (The rankness of Cousin Ethel, the fetidness of piss steaming up from the furnace, and the exotic spice of incense; the soapy smell of scrubbed surfaces, the fragrance of baking bread, the scent of ripe apples.) The mad conglomeration of beliefs from my childhood: tepid Mormonism, Catholic mysticism, cynicism. The unshakable faith of Norma's family.

Being caught in the maelstrom of the straits between her heritage and her husband, Norma was deeply troubled, a state of affairs aggravated by what we ultimately learned was a genetic tendency to clinical depression, now controlled with medication. Nonetheless, Norma went through hell, and I won't even attempt to express my sorrow over the part that I played in her troubles. (So desperate was her situation that the word *troubles* is inadequate.)

As Norma struggled to maintain her own sanity, she was therapy for me, and I began to gain a bit of equilibrium, even peace. One result of my renascence, or perhaps the cause of it, was the warmth that I began to feel for Norma's family, particularly her mother. Marcella was a second-generation Swede, ungiven to displays of affection, appearing standoffish, aloof, but as she and I began to develop our friendship, I learned that beneath that starchy exterior was endless love and understanding and a surprising ability to have fun—surprising at least to me. I remember one of her visits to us in Southern California after Maitland died. On a day when Norma had her own commitments, Marcella and I went out on a date. We took a boat tour of the Newport back bay, with its multimillion dollar homes and its yachts. As we were having lunch at an outdoor restaurant on Balboa Island, Marcella said to me, "This is the first time I've eaten at an outdoor restaurant."

As I grew closer to Norma's family, I began to understand and appreciate Mormon culture, particularly the stress on family. In the Graham home, Norma had experienced the security and stability that were never a part of my childhood. In that home, she had learned and lived a rich culture: music, for each of the eight children played at least one instrument; song; handicrafts such as knitting and crocheting; a nearness to and love of the earth and its bounties; and poetry, Edgar Guest being the laureate.

Is it perfume from a dress that makes me so digress? One hallmark of my maturity and sanity is that I can *now* view the poetry of Edgar Guest as a part of a rich culture. When I first became a member-by-marriage of the Graham clan, I sneered at most aspects of their culture, in particular the literature that made up their library, not only Edgar Guest, but dozens of books authored by the authorities of the Mormon Church: autobiographies, professions of faith, commentaries on doctrine. For example, I inherited: *Gospel Ideals: Selections from the Discourses of David O. McKay, Ninth President of the Church of Jesus Christ of Latter Day Saints*, an Improvement Era Publication, 1953, inscribed "Merry Christmas to Mom and Dad from [daughter] Beulah and [her husband] Eldon, [son] Ken and [his wife] Julia, Norma and Ross, [daughter] Eva and [her husband] Dale 1953." How could a person whose own icons included T. S. Eliot and James Joyce have any reaction but scorn for the Graham taste in literature? I now wonder why I spent so much of my life reading "correct" texts, including that lugubrious triviality, Restoration drama. The yield for me in pleasure and wisdom was minimal. The Graham culture was much richer than my own, but it took decades for me to realize this.

Through the years, as I read the Mormon scriptures and discussed the religion with my in-laws, I became more and more alienated from the church's doctrine. Though I will not launch upon an extended discussion of Mormonism, I must say that orthodox believers have always puzzled me, for they must either ignore historical fact (e.g., the indisputable fact that one of their sacred texts, Joseph Smith's "translation" of "The Book of Abraham" from "reformed Egyptian," is a hoax) or rationalize contradictions that to me are insuperable. However, several of my close friends are devout but unorthodox Mormons, realizing the problems with the sacred texts and the history of the Church, but living in and loving the Mormon culture. As a member of Clan Graham, I can understand this.

The most significant influence on my religious beliefs and my quest for faith has been my younger son, Reverend Anthony G. Winterowd, D.Min. In some ways, religion has driven us farther apart, but in many ways it has brought us closer together.

From the point of view of his parents, Tony's religious life began suddenly one day when he was a freshman or sophomore in high school. Without any preliminaries, without having been a church goer, he announced to us that he wanted to be baptized. We, of course, gave him our (secular) blessing, and he was baptized by immersion in the First Christian Church of Huntington Beach. He went on to take a bachelor's degree in religion at the University of Southern California, a master's at Biola University, and his doctorate in ministry at Talbot, Biola's theological seminary. He is now pastor in the First Presbyterian Church of Hanford, California.

Since we have always been close to our two sons (Geoffrey, now an attorney practicing in Pasadena, and Tony}, it was inevitable that I should begin to think about and investigate religion. First I read the Bible. Becoming fascinated by that endlessly rich text, I started to read studies of the Bible; histories of Christianity; and such canonical texts as Augustine's *Confessions* and *City of God* and Aquinas's *Summa Theologiciæ*.

For the last five or six years, I have been interested in religion; for the last three years, I have been immersed in the subject. Since this book is an attempt to explain my own faith and beliefs, I won't say anything about them now, except that they diverge radically from the faith and beliefs of my son, a difference that in our case powers ongoing dialogue.

From my Mormon in-laws and from my theological son, I have learned one great lesson: genuine love supersedes religious beliefs and politics. My brothers-in-law Ken and Gaylen are the staunchest of staunch Mormons—and two of my dearest friends. My son is the staunchest of staunch conservative Presbyterians—and he is one of my very dearest friends.

How shall I now say what I want to say? Bluntly, I suppose. When my religious odyssey began with my marriage in 1952, I was neurotic and more than slightly paranoid. I realize now that I knew no peace; my life was frenzy. I didn't really enjoy literature even though I had to profess my love for the texts that I was writing about and teaching. Packed into the following anecdote is a great deal of the meaning of my life just at the beginning of my religious "conversion."

In 1952 and 1953, thanks to a Fulbright Scholarship, Norma and I honeymooned in Vienna, a city recovering from the war and not yet Americanized. Fairview and McGill were transported to one of the cultural centers of the Old World. No McDonald's, no Kleenex, no Franco-American canned spaghetti. Schinkenwurst, Ementhaler, newspaper squares in the WC. The Kunsthistorisches Museum, with its dozen or so Brueghels and its Titians and Franz Hals. The Vienna Philharmonic orchestra, and the Volksoper for operetta and the Staatsoper for grand opera. We knew that, *de rigueur*, we should purchase a subscription to a series of Philharmonic concerts. Norma wanted the Romantische Musik series: Brahm's, Beethoven, Mendelsohn, Schubert, Tchaikovsky. However, Romanticism was out of fashion in the literary world; Wordsworth, Coleridge, Byron, Keats, and Shelley were for wimps, for readers who wallowed in sentimentality and completely lacked the acuity to appreciate wit. Restoration drama and metaphysical poetry were in: the dreary cynicism of, for instance, *The Way of the World* and the metaphorical paradoxes of John Donne, Richard Crashaw, and Andrew Marvell, poets that I still read with joy, but poets world's apart from the Romantics. Concomitant with literary fashion were the approved composers: Bach, Haydn, Händel, Mozart. Norma, of course, with her rural tastes and lack of literary sophistication, opted for the Romantic series. I can't remember exactly what I said to her—probably something like, "I don't want to drown in a sea of treacle or feast on cotton candy." We purchased the Baroque series. I squirmed through the concerts; Norma enjoyed them.

The faith that I have found comes from my relationships with those I love and from the books that have affected me so deeply as to have become part of my intellect and my beliefs. Thus, the story I am going to tell will be "bookish," but not, I hope, pedantic. The one book that has been most powerful in my life since I began my quest is, of course, the Bible, but other texts have had a strong influence: Augustine's *Confessions*; William James's *Pragmatism*; John Dewey's *A Common Faith*; *Moby Dick*; *The Brothers Karamazov*; Wallace Stevens's poems; Tolstoy's *Resurrection*; Peter Matthiessen's *The Snow Leopard*; the poems of Walt Whitman. And others.

My confession is nearly done. In the early morning or late evening hours, I have probed more deeply than I am willing to do in this public statement. I cannot utter my regrets, for there are no words to express them. Nor are my unuttered laments grand or tragic, merely the sorrow of one whose time is running short and who seeks ways of atonement.

And finally, a story about hiking.

For years and years, Norma and I hiked; it was our passion, our release, and our greatest pleasure. It is also our most poignant memory, for in 1999, Norma suffered a disastrous stroke, ending for the rest of our lives the hikes that were so wonderful a part of our life together.

We hiked the Appalachian trail in several places, one in the White Mountains of Maine in late summer; along the trail were wild raspberry bushes, and we spent more time picking and eating the ripe berries than we did moving up the trail. On another occasion, we hiked out of Roanoke and gained enough altitude to look out over the autumn colors of maple, larch, and oak, the ocean of brilliance in the afternoon sun of late September. With dear friends, we hiked in early November among the mists and the silver, leafless birches on the north shore of Lake Superior.

But year after year, we made the pilgrimage to hike on and up Mount Wheeler in Great Basin National Park, south of Ely, Nevada, and nearly on the Utah border. The boundary of the park is in the sagebrush flats, stretches of territory with their own austere beauty. But when the road begins to climb Mount Wheeler, the scenery becomes alpine, with aspens, piñon, and ponderosa, and just at timber line, the ancient bristlecones. In the cirque of the mountain is the southernmost glacier on the North American continent.

At the foot of the Mountain are Lehman Caves, an extensive and spectacular series of caverns. On one of our visits to the Park, we decided to go through the caves with a park ranger. We being the only tourists that day, the ranger asked if we would like to see the cave as Absalom Lehman had when he discovered it in 1885. We eagerly agreed and were given tin-can lanterns lit by candles. We saw the wonders of the caverns by the dim, flickering light and followed the warp of time back for a hundred or so years.

After having toured the cave, we drove up and up the serpentine road leading to the trailhead at 10,000 feet. We hiked through pine almost to timberline and to the bristlecone forest, the most gnarled, tenacious flora in the world (except, possibly, for the California creosote bush). And then we hiked on to the glacier.

A poem that I wrote tells about that hike and gives the clearest statement I can make about my idea of heaven.

> With candles groping down through Lehman Cave,
> We chased the shadows of reality
> And saw the cavern as Ab Lehman had.
> The flicker led him back and back toward
> A treasure. In the greatest Saal he dreamed
> A courtly dance, the fiddles tuning up,
> Their echoes crinoline and riding boots.[2]
>
> Emerging in the blaring sun, we blinked
> And wiped our eyes; newborn, we tottered stunned,
> Our bleary gaze toward the misted peak.
>
> An easy climb through pine and aspen glades.
> I watched the muscles flexing in her legs,
> Her working buttocks tight within her shorts,
> And heard her breathing deeply in thin air,
> The quartz shards clinking with her every step.
>
> When we reached the bristlecones, we paused
> To ponder those tenacious trees, so gnarled,
> But not eternal, no, yet nearly so
> As anything on earth. The cones were bright
> With golden honey, fecund, pregnant, ripe.
>
> We ate our M&Ms in pinescent air
> And sipped the lukewarm water from canteens.

Above the timber, scrambling through the scree,
We reached the cirque, the glistening our goal,
Then crunched through ice upon the glacier's face,
And on the farther side, sat peacefully.

We'll take the hike again, again, perhaps,
But someday we'll just stay there, glacier-bound,
Side by side, thinking of the bristlecones,
The M&Ms, the water, and the scree.

2

Prayer

> Unto Him is the real prayer. Those unto whom they pray beside Allah respond to them not at all, save as (is the response to) one who stretcheth forth his hands toward water (asking) that it may come unto his mouth and it will never reach it. The prayer of disbelievers goeth (far) astray.
>
> —*Koran* 13:14

I am not a frequent or consistent pray-er; I do not bless the food or say evening or morning or bedtime prayers. I suspect that for most pray-ers, praying is a routine, like saying "Excuse me" after eructation. Yet prayer fascinates me, and I have prayed.

It is axiomatic that every sincere prayer is answered. If you are a believer in a god who can intervene to change the course of events and you ask that god to intervene, then you know that he (He?) will answer your prayer. Thus, as a farmer you pray for rain, and the rain comes. Your prayer has been answered. You then pray that the price of wheat will rise, and the price falls. Your prayer has been answered. God has given you a message, perhaps about greed. Or he has taught you a lesson about destiny. Or you have learned that the ways of God are inscrutable—even though you know, as a believer, that all is for the ultimate good. In any case, you, as a committed believer, have received god's answer to your prayer.

In its article on "prayer," *Encyclopedia Britannica* lists the following types: petition, asking for personal benefits, either spiritual or material; intercession, asking God (or the gods) to intervene in human affairs as praying that the deity bring about peace; praise and thanksgiving; adoration, "a kind of prostration of the whole being before God"; and unitative, to achieve mystical union with God, oneness with the deity.

I would add two more types to the list in the *Britannica*: prayers of desperation and prayers that attempt to say the unsayable.

It was midnight or after. My wife, Norma, lay in the hospital bed with catheters and IVs either dripping fluids into her or draining fluids out. She was desperately ill. Her physician had said only that the prognosis was not favorable. In fact, her muscles were dissolving and passing out through her urine.

That afternoon, I had fallen from my bicycle and had injured my left leg, an extremely painful contusion and sprain which made it impossible for me to be comfortable on the cot that the hospital had provided. And, now as I attempt to tell this story, I realize how insignificant my discomfort was, except that it was part of a syndrome of desperation.

Norma and I both, unfashionably, enjoy Delius, so to give her whatever pleasure (distraction? comfort?) I could, I had brought a portable radio with a CD player and a couple of disks of Delius. We had listened to this music for an hour or so, its tranquility flowing over us, not an anodyne, but a spectral wisp of the days and years when the music of Delius was background for dining or reading or, in Norma's case, for knitting. We had never taken Delius seriously, any more than we take seriously the mystery shows to which we are addicted. But now the music was a background for mortality and was no longer Muzak; it spoke of life's passing and of years and years of companionship. In that room in the hospital, Delius carried, for us, as much meaning as Verdi's *Requiem* (one of Norma's most beloved works).

And Norma was dying.

From the hall outside the dark room, a buzzer, then a laugh, then silence, then the sound of vacuum cleaner, then silence.

And Norma was dying.

I twisted on the cot, trying to get comfortable. A nurse opened the door a crack, peeked into the room, and then, without entering, shut the door again.

And Norma was dying.

She was wasting away, unable even to raise her arm or to shift positions in her bed. She moaned, and I rolled off the cot, my leg throbbing, and massaged her legs and turned her onto her side and massaged her buttocks. She seemed to be soothed. I got back onto the cot and returned to the black meditation that had replaced sleep.

The thoughts I had were sometimes embarrassingly mundane. *Now I'll sell the house. I'll burn the place down. Can't stand the thought of packing things up or giving things away. I'll just disappear and let our sons worry about the house and its contents.*

And sometimes my thoughts were sepulchral. *Cremation. Some kind of memorial service. I'll just have everyone sit and listen to Verdi's Requiem. Let the boys handle everything. I'm going to Nevada to be alone in Great Basin National Park.*

But the hardest moments, almost unbearable, were when I relived our life together. The first year of marriage, our honeymoon" in Vienna on a Fulbright. The army years in Stuttgart. Erbsen Suppe mit Wurst for a few cents in the third class restaurant at the Bahnhof. The births of our sons and our grandsons. Taking our grandson Chris to Italy, his first trip abroad.

Spontaneously in these dark hours, I said to myself, "God, please preserve her." What could that mean? I, who don't believe that a deity intervenes in human affairs. It was a prayer of desperation, an inevitable *cri de coeur* that, were I a believer, might have been a curse. I had reached the end of hope, and my prayer—if the utterance *was* a prayer—was automatic, spontaneous, a reflex. But no less a welling up from my very depths. It was a prayer of desperation.

Norma survived. As a cynic, I might say ironically, "You see, my prayer worked." And what would I say if Norma had died? That God hadn't heard my prayer? That saving Norma at that time was not part of His universal plan? That He was punishing me for my skepticism?

In fact, there was nothing to say. The prayer was simply part of that nightmare, as was my injured leg.

In his novel *Resurrection*, Tolstoy's protagonist, the roué Nekhlyudov, has seduced a young woman, who in desperation becomes a prostitute and is then falsely convicted of murder and sentenced to penal servitude in Siberia. At the time of the sentencing, he has an awakening of conscience.

> He stopped, crossed his hand over his breast as he used to do when he was a child, lifted his eyes and said, addressing someone:
>
> "O Lord, help me, instruct me, come and take Thine abode in me and cleanse me from all impurity." (142)

This is a prayer of desperation much like my prayer for Norma's deliverance. After the prayer, Nekhlyudov felt himself at one with God. "All, all the best a man could do, he now felt himself capable of doing." However, this sense of holy nobility shares Nekhlyudov's spiritual being with a corrupt ego, and Tolstoy's comments are devastating:

> His eyes filled with tears as he was saying all this to himself, good and bad tears: good because they were tears of joy at the awakening of the spiritual being within him, the being that had slumbered all these years; and bad tears of tender emotion at his own goodness. (142)

In this scene, Tolstoy captures the ambivalence of prayer, of my prayer for Norma and of your prayers for yourself and those you love.

There are limits to *sayability*, language being able to go only so far in expressing ideas and feelings. Society imposes one sort of limit. There are words that are unsayable and ideas that are unexpressible *within given cultural situations*. For years, I played the game of "chicken" to illustrate this principle for my students. The game was simple. I would write words on the blackboard, one after another, and when the class could no longer bear to read and to hear me pronounce the next one, the students should raise their hands to stop me from writing it. "Heck." No response. "Hell." No response. "Shit." Some obvious uneasiness and a hand or two. "Sonofabitch." More uneasiness, and more hands. And then the first letter "F." The word doesn't get written out. All of the hands go up. In the context of my classroom at the University of Southern California, the F-word, so common around campus and certainly in the dorms, was unsayable publicly.

Some feelings and senses (and I wish there were better terms) are not expressible in ordinary language (awe, despair, joy, wonder, love, hate), which is the reason for poetry, music, and painting. In *Women in Love* and *Lady Chatterley's Lover*, D. H. Lawrence said as much as he could about his eroticism, but there was an excess of meaning that he poured into his paintings, particularly one haunting work, "Red Willows," in which a nude male figure, viewed from behind, crouches, his buttocks forming a perfect image of the glans of a penis. Or Beethoven's choral symphony, the "Ode to Joy." Or Goya's "Black Paintings from the Quinta del Sordo." Or Wallace Stevens's poem about Saint Ursula.[3] Or one of the profoundly great American books, *The Snow Leopard*, by Peter Matthiessen. Much of art is the attempt to say the unsayable. And so I think are many prayers, such as the one I tell about in the following entry from my journal..

> On an airplane, Orlando-LA
> November 2, 1994
>
> Manuel was a particularly gifted student, an outgoing, warm, friendly young man who had emigrated—legally, I think—from Guatemala. His English was remarkably fluent, and he was doing excellent work in my senior-level linguistics class.

Keen-minded, witty, and very gentle, Manuel was clearly the star among the twenty-five students in the class—yet early in the semester I began to sense an ominous wasting away of his already-thin body and a progressively deepening hollowness in his eyes, though his endless good humor and affability did not change.

Manuel was a frequent visitor to my office, where we would talk about the class, about his home in Guatemala, and about life in general, particularly his amazement at the casual attitudes of students at the University of Southern California, for he took education very seriously.

I knew that something was drastically wrong with him, and I suspected what it was, for my wife and I had seen a close friend waste into a skeletal wraith, AIDS gnawing at him like maggots, yet I had no warrant to broach the subject of illness to Manuel and no right to encroach on his privacy. Chemotherapy had left him completely bald, and sitting in class was obviously painful, if not agonizing.

Then came the day when Manuel peeked into my office and waited for me to invite him in.

"Professor Winterowd," he said, "I must talk to you"—and for ten or fifteen minutes, not whiningly, not melodramatically, but with quiet resignation and dignity, he told of the problems of facing death. "I needed to say this to you," he told me, and as he rose to leave my office, he handed me a small cross carved from bone, painted with a red and black design, and hung on a black string.

The semester ended. I called Manuel often, and my wife and I took him to lunch at our favorite Chinese restaurant. When we were seated, Manuel explained his embarrassment: if he removed his cap, everyone would see his baldness, but to leave his cap on would be discourteous to his hosts. We solved the problem. I too left my cap on.

A day or two after the Chinese meal, I called Manuel's number, but there was no answer. Manuel was gone. Whether he died in a hospice or alone or had a funeral or where he was buried, we did not know. Manuel was gone, and I only knew that I loved him and would cherish his memory.

That year, my wife, my theological son, and I vacationed on the Florida and Georgia coasts, as always talking heavy theology hour after hour, for there is no escaping our son's interest and commitment. Quite by chance, in St. Augustine we wandered into a Greek Orthodox chapel. Though I know little about the Eastern Rite, I have a particular love for Byzantine art, especially icons, with their haunting, other-worldly portrayal of Christ, the Disciples, and the Saints, in gold, crimson, and blue robes with their pale, almost translucent flesh contrasted with the ebony of the wood panels on which they are painted. On another trip, my wife and I had seen the icon collection in the Byzantine Museum in Athens; we had experienced the luminosity of mosaic icons in the Monastery of Hosias Lucas, between Delphi (one of the holiest sites in Western civilization) and Athens; and we had bought our son an icon that now hangs in his office at his church.

All of this merely to explain why the Greek chapel in St. Augustine was so significant to me.

As I strolled about, holy chants echoing softly, a feeling came over me, a sense of deep sadness that was yet peaceful. I felt I must respond somehow to what I was experiencing: my love for my wife and son and my joy at being with them; the familiar and personally meaningful beauty of the chapel; and, above all, my sense of loss, the passing of a brilliant young man with whom I had developed a unique relationship.

I prayed to express what is actually beyond expression in any way but, perhaps, through art and music or through reverential silence. I said words, but I have no idea what they were, and their exact nature is, in any case, irrelevant.

At the end of my prayer, which must have been brief, perhaps a minute or so, I had the deep sense that I was one with the universe and that the universe is not meaningless. I can say no more about the experience, but I do have thoughts about its significance.

In the first place, I wish that I could have shared the experience with Manuel. I think this would have helped him. Furthermore, I know that my prayer or any other would have had no effect on the course of Manuel's ultimate destiny.

Now then, what did I learn from this experience? Did it prove anything? How can I prove its reality to you?

I gained a deep kind of personal knowledge that results only from experience. The texture of dreams is incommunicable; the electricity of the act of love is indescribable. There are realms of very real experience that are and always will be personal and unsharable by any vicarious means. Such is the nature of what I would call "true prayers." There is no way for the skeptic to deny the experience of others, and there is no way for the "believer" to convince the skeptic. Yet the personal insight and experience, the mystic vision, is the very foundation of religion—not "empirical" evidence and not "logic" (whatever that might be). Theology (i.e., knowledge about God) relies on historicity, epistemologies, and philosophies; belief (i.e., knowledge of God) results from personal experience.

So I'm talking about two realms of knowledge, which we might call the "personal" and the "public." A person with the deepest faith (i.e., personal knowledge) might also want to know theology, in which case this person. . . . But why go on? I'll conclude thus: the bone cross that Manuel gave me still hangs in my study, and I treasure it.

What might be called the "literary prayer" should also be added to the typology. I find this kind of prayer deeply satisfying. It has a dual nature, as prayer and as work of art, such as Donne's "Holy Sonnet XIV":

> Batter my heart, three-personed God; for You
> As yet but knock, breathe, shine, and seek to mend;
> That I may rise and stand, o'erthrow me, and bend
> Your force, to break, blow, burn, and make me new.
> I, like an usurped town, to another due,
> Labor to admit You, but Oh, to no end!
> Reason, Your viceroy in me, me should defend,
> But is captived, and proves weak or untrue.
> Yet dearly I love You, and would be loved fain,
> But am betrothed unto Your enemy:
> Divorce me, untie or break that knot again,
> Take me to You, imprison me, for I,
> Except You enthrall me, never shall be free,
> Nor ever chaste, except You ravish me.

I will sidestep the issue of poetic school and genre into which the sonnet falls, for that literary and historical information is beside my point. It *is* a prayer, and what I'm getting at is the revolutionary, unsettling nature of imagery, which is so daring that it might well offend many believers—and so daring that it might open whole new realms of understanding for believers.

First, the poet-prayer invokes the terrible God of the Old Testament, asking this deity to force, break, blow, burn, and make new, replacing the gentle kindness of the God who knocks, breathes, shines, and seeks to mend. Donne is begging Yahweh-Elohim to replace Christ, thus evoking the enigmatic duality of the Old Testament and the New Testament God.

Now comes the first of two daring images: that of the usurped town under siege, a secular and perhaps sinful place: Jericho, Sodom, Gomorrah. Immured in this unholy city, the pray-er finds himself powerless; even his reason, God's viceroy, is captive and is weak and untrue.

The dilemma is that the pray-er, captive in the profane city, longs for divine love: "Yet dearly I love You, and would be loved fain." The introduction of that word "love" brings about a radical shift in the prayer-poem, certainly one of the most daring metaphors in metaphysical poetry, God becoming a ravisher in both the unholy (sexual) and the holy (spiritual) sense. In the worldly city, the poet is betrothed to Satan and begs God, "Divorce me, untie or break that knot again." And then the double paradox: the poet can never be free unless *enthralled* by God and never chaste unless *ravished* by God. The ambiguity of those terms *enthrall* and *ravish* points in two directions: toward the sacred and toward the profane, the poet, like other mortals, caught inexorably between the two. To *enthrall* is either to hold spellbound or to enslave; to *ravish* is to seize and carry away by force, to rape or violate, or to enrapture.

This sonnet-prayer, I think, solves no theological problems, offers no easy consolation, indeed troubles the careful reader, leaves him or her to contemplate the mysteries of God's relationship to humankind. Whether humans are bodies animated by spirit or spirits imprisoned in bodies, we are doomed to the sort of ambiguity expressed in the sonnet, and that is, for me, as much of a lesson as I can gain from the poem, but that is more than enough.

I find that prayers, if they are not from reflex and habit, are often as morally ambiguous as life itself. An example of such an ambiguous prayer is from Kathleen Norris's *The Cloister Walk*, a journal of the author's experiences and thoughts during her two nine-month terms as an oblate at St. John's Abbey in Collegeville, Minnesota. Here is one complete entry, for February 10, titled "Scholastica":

> One winter night, Benedict's sister, Scholastica,[4] was awakened by a song bird. How can this be, she thought, and she looked out the window of her cell. Three naked men were dancing in the monastery garden by the light of the moon. One whistled like a bird and made her laugh. The men were

fair to look at, Scholastica thought, but she knew she needed more rest before the first prayers of the day.

Kneeling by her bed, she closed her eyes and sleepily said a prayer for the men—if they were men—that they might find shelter, clothing, and rest for their dancing feet, and if (as she suspected) they were demons, that they might return to from whence they came.

When she awoke, her cell was filled with the scent of roses. Where the men had been dancing a rose bush had sprung up and was blooming in the snow. It bloomed all that winter, and it blooms to this day. (124)

In our post-Freudian world, we can interpret the tale as a fantasy rising in the mind of a sexually repressed neurotic, but that, it seems to me, is vandalistic. I prefer the ambiguity of the naked dancers: deranged humans or demons seducing the innocent. In either case, the rosebush is a fitting tribute from the Lord to an infinitely faithful and loving servant.

The imagery of the text is unforgettable: the cell, the naked men dancing in the moonlight, the rosebush. How wonderful the laconic remark "but she knew she needed more rest before the first prayers of the day." First things first. The figures, whether human or diabolic, were less important than preparation for devotions. And Scholastica, in her unshakable faith, does not trouble herself with questions about the humanity or inhumanity of the dancers, merely hoping that, if they are human, they find shelter.

Yet we are troubled by Scholastica's lack of concern. If the dancers were human, why not offer them shelter. If they were demonic, why be so unconcerned? Do the routines of devotion such as prayers and mass supersede human and divine questions? Think of the image: Scholastica experiences the supernatural, but is concerned only about getting enough sleep. Does Scholastica's prayer reveal faith or complacency?

And, of course, prayer is marketable. Stripped of its ambiguity, its mystery, its beauty, and (I must say, it's reverence and awe), prayer becomes theological junk food—quick and easy; not nutritious; and causing, in some with weak constitutions such as mine, spiritual and intellectual dyspepsia. I find these marketable, junk-food prayers to be distasteful. In fact, I abhor them.

In December, 2001, a book about prayer was number one on the *New York Times* best-seller "advice" list: *The Prayer of Jabez*, by Bruce Wilkinson is a ninety-three-pager that capitalizes on the interest that the public has in prayer. Available in addition to the original hardcover are *The Prayer of Jabez Leather Edition*, *The Prayer of Jabez Journal*, *The Prayer of Jabez Devotional*, *The Prayer of Jabez Bible Study*, *The Prayer of Jabez for Teens*, and *The Prayer of Jabez Gift Edition*.

Wilkinson bases *The Prayer of Jabez* on a brief passage from 1 Chronicles 4:9–10.

> Now Jabez was more honorable than his brothers, and his mother called his name Jabez, saying, "Because I bore him in pain." And Jabez called on the God of Israel saying, "Oh, that You would bless me indeed, and enlarge my territory, that Your hand would be with me, and that you would keep me from evil, that I may not cause pain!" So God granted him what he requested.

The story begins, Wilkinson tells us, on a rainy afternoon in Dallas as he and his wife Darlene are pondering what his future should be. He has finished seminary. One of his seminary professors had challenged him to be "a gimper for God" (9), a gimper being a person who does just a little extra, who goes a distance beyond the call of duty, and the professor had taken as his text the passage about Jabez from 1 Chronicles. At this crucial moment in his life, Wilkinson remembers the prayer of Jabez, and he prays it.

For thirty years, Wilkinson tells us, he has been repeating that prayer. He wants to introduce you "to the amazing truths in Jabez's prayer for blessing and prepare you to expect God's astounding answers to it *as a regular part of your life experience*" (11).

This little book is a perfect example of a type in American popular theology: treatises on the use of prayer for success, material more than spiritual. The archetype is Bruce Barton's *The Man Nobody Knows*, about which I will remark shortly. Another is *Prayer: My Soul's Adventure with God*, by Robert H. Schuler, and yet another is *Our Search for Happiness*, by M. Russell Ballard.

Here is *The Prayer of Jabez* in abstract.

Chapter 1 "Little Prayer, Giant Prize" (*Jabez called on the God of Israel.*) And the prizes are beyond doubt. At one time, Wilkinson was teaching the prayer to an audience of 9,000, and over lunch a member of his audience said to him, "Bruce, I heard you preach the message of Jabez fifteen years ago, and I haven't stopped praying it. The change has been so overwhelming I have just never stopped" (16). And a heart surgeon across the table seconded the endorsement. The Prayer of Jabez pays off.

Chapter 2 "So Why Not Ask?" (*Oh, that you would bless me indeed!*) Greed is good! "Is it possible," Wilkinson asks, " that God wants you to be 'selfish' in your prayers?" (19). God has an eternal warehouse packed with blessings just waiting to be requested through prayer. "Even though there is no limit to God's goodness, if you didn't ask Him for a blessing yesterday, you didn't get all that you were supposed to have" (27). Those blessings, of course, might be success in a properly conducted business, but also the restoring of lost souls to the flock. If your heart is right, commerce and communion are indistinguishable.

Chapter 3 "Living Large for God" (*Oh, that you would enlarge my territory!*) In the tradition of Bruce Barton, founder of the mighty BBDO ad agency and author of the 1925 best-selling life of Christ, *The Man Nobody Knows*, Wilkinson sets forth a Christian rationalization for commerce.

Wilkinson tells us that "If Jabez had worked on Wall Street, he might have prayed, 'Lord, increase the value of my investment portfolios'" (31). When presidents of companies ask Wilkinson if it's right to pray for more business, Wilkinson assures them that God is just waiting for them to ask. After all, "To pray for larger borders is to ask for a miracle—it's that simple" (43). And there's really nothing so miraculous about miracles. "[M]iracles don't have to break natural law to be a supernatural event. When Christ stilled the storm, He didn't set aside natural law—the storm would eventually have subsided on its own. Instead, he directed the weather pattern" (43).[5]

Chapter 4 "The Touch of Greatness" (*Oh, that your hand would be with me!*); Chapter 5 "Keeping the Legacy Safe" (*Oh, that you would keep me from evil!*); and Chapter 6 "Welcome to God's Honor Roll" (*Jabez was more honorable than his brothers!*) tell us that God will make (commercial) heroes out of ordinary mortals, will protect us from Satan's power, and will hold back "nothing from those who want and earnestly long for what He wants" (76). And Wilkinson gives an example of how God works for those who ask his blessings.

> I was driving through Atlanta to the airport on my way to an important speaking engagement in North Carolina. Without warning, traffic slowed, then stopped. A major accident had blocked all lanes. When it became clear that I was going to miss my flight, I prayed, "Lord, please make my flight late so I can catch it." (79)

When he arrived at the concourse for departure, he found that "Sure enough, the flight had been delayed" (79). Wilkinson does not go on to speculate about the inconveniences, annoyances, or even tragedies the delay might have caused other passengers.

Wilkinson's book is in the tradition of Bruce Barton's *The Man Nobody Knows*, the great American commercial interpretation of the life of Jesus. In Chapter 10, "Christianity and Capitalism," I will have more to say about Barton.

I'd like to conclude this chapter with some remarks about a book by a friend and former colleague, *The Divine Conspiracy*, by Dallas

Willard, who defines prayer as "Talking to God about what we are doing together" (243). Dallas's book is one of a kind: the down-to-earth confession of a mystic in the sense that devoted Christianity is a sort of mysticism. Much popular Christian literature (such as *The Prayer of Jabez*) focuses on what God can do for you and how to get Him to do it; *The Divine Conspiracy* is a book about living a life with God and in God.

I had read the book a couple of years ago and had simply forgotten the theological argument that constitutes the superstructure: the religious right claims salvation through "an *arrangement* for forgiveness of sin" (49), making the living presence of Christ irrelevant, and the religious left substitutes social action for the relationship with Christ (50–55). Dallas would bring Christians from both right and left back into what I can only call the mystical union with God.

Though I had forgotten the argument, what I did remember from the book, what lived vividly in my memory, was Dallas's account of praying. His prayers are, to refer back to the *Britannica* categories, *unitative*. Here is his experience with "The Lord's Prayer":

> [T]here were many nights when I would awaken about two o'clock and spend an hour of delight before God just dwelling in one or more phrases from it. I had to make a point at times, as I still do, of praying thoughtfully on *through* the entire prayer. Otherwise the riches of one or two phrases in the prayer would be all I could develop, and I would not benefit from all its contents. (268)

If I were a pray-er, that is the kind of prayer I would like to offer up. But I am not a pray-er. Prayer has given me no help in my search for faith.

Yet each night before I go to sleep, I silently ask a blessing for those I love.

3

Seeking Faith: Scripture

> Then one of the seraphs flew to me. [. . .] And he
> said, "Go and say to this people:
> 'Keep listening, but do not comprehend;
> Keep looking, but do not understand.'
>
> —*Isaiah* 6

My search for faith began with the Bible. I had no hope of a beatific vision, but I did and do know that the Holy Bible is the rock upon which believers (such as my son and daughter-in-law) build their citadels of faith. My problem is that I came to the Bible as a reader, not as a believer—and that makes an enormous difference. By the time my three-year-old grandson is ready to read the Bible, he will know with rock-solid certainty that it is true and the word of God. I came to the Bible as a skeptic, looking for faith, not as a believer, reaffirming my faith.

As a reader, not as a believer, I found the Bible to be the most engaging and frustrating and paradoxical text I had ever encountered. In my three years of reading, I developed a love-hate relationship with the Bible; its enigmas gnawed at me; its glories left me elated; its banalities disgusted me; its long passages of finicky (and nutty, insane) law-giving bored me; its subtle undertones of sexuality and evil fascinated me. The Bible engaged me as it has so many readers through the centuries. And, of course, I have my own interpretations of this and that and of the whole *book*. The Bible *is* a book!

What we can rationally do is take a look at what happens when people read a text and then conclude, with me, I hope, that interpretation is tenuous and personal and that dogmatic solutions to questions of Biblical interpretation only create more enmity and dividedness.

Four Fundamentals

I begin with what I take to be obvious: To understand scripture, one must read it. The seeker after truth cannot merely clasp the Bible, *The Book of Mormon*, or the Koran to his or her chest and wait for meaning and spiritual insight to emanate from the volume into the soul and mind (as my mother used to believe that the essences of Musterole penetrated my chest and drew out the congestion, thus relieving the cold). It goes without saying, of course, that my priest or spiritual adviser might explain scripture to me, thus making it unnecessary for me to read the text. However, in that case, I am understanding the spiritual adviser, not scripture—which creates a whole new problem, one that I will deal with only tangentially.

Granted, reading scripture has dimensions beyond those that map out the territory of ordinary reading—the daily newspaper, a poem by Keats, a novel by Dickens, a legal code, a set of instructions. However, *all* reading entails certain essentials.

1. *Reading a text is an attempt to make sense of an entirety, to understand the parts as they contribute to the coherence of the whole.* One cannot *read War and Peace* by dipping in here and there, even on a regular basis. ("Have you read *Paradise Lost*?" "Oh yes, I choose five lines at random every night before I go to sleep.") A text such as *War and Peace* or the Bible is not of the same genre as an encyclopedia; one does not read the *Britannica*, but one *does* read entries in the encyclopedia in their entirety.

   One can, of course, read parts of the Bible without relating them to the whole. Thus, the book of Job can stand alone and has done so in college literature courses; however, a reader who considers the Bible to be a unified work, not simply an anthology, must relate the parts—the book of Job, a psalm, the "Song of Solomon"—to the whole.

Bible samplers who do not attempt to put the whole work together are a danger, for one can find warrant for any absurdity or atrocity in not only the Bible, but probably in any scripture.

2. *The human mind and sensoria predetermine what and how one can read.* I am told that the dream in which one flies is common, but the reality is that one cannot flap one's arms and glide off like the lark ascending. I cannot read a text in a language with which I am totally unfamiliar—even if I resort to dictionaries and other reference sources. Once I have transliterated the text, then *perhaps* I can read it, but a word-for-word transliteration does not constitute reading. If one knows the Cyrillic alphabet, one can, after a fashion, pronounce the words in a Russian text, but pronouncing is not reading, for reading is deriving meaning. That is, my ability to pronounce is not necessary to my ability to read, and my ability to read is not necessary to my ability to pronounce (though the two are most frequently coincidental). (See the first essential, above.)

3. *Every text (whether the Bible, The Book of Mormon, the Koran, or other) is culturally situated, both in its genesis and in its reconstitution by a reader.* Massive scholarship at least partially establishes the cultural genesis of the Bible, but just as complex as the historical question is that of the cultural situation of the reader. Works such as Augustine's *Confessions* and Newman's *Apologia pro vita sua* can be read as studies in the relationship between culture and faith. People who read the Bible prior to 1859, the year in which Darwin published *Origin of Species*, were in a radically different cultural situation from those who read the Bible after 1859, regardless of their individual views regarding the validity of Darwin's

theories and regardless of whether or not these readers had firsthand knowledge of Darwin's work.

4. *It is clearly demonstrable that interpreters can agree on the meanings of texts.* This in effect means that texts can be, and frequently are, at least momentarily determinate. However, agreement among a group of readers on *the* meaning of a text is a fragile construct that often shatters the moment someone asks a question about *the* meaning on which *everyone* agrees. For example, "everyone" agrees that God created the earth from nothingness—or at least "everyone" agrees until someone like Karen Armstrong begins questioning. The first sentence of Genesis, she tells us, is often translated as "In the beginning God created heaven and earth." However, the inexorable ambiguity of language can deconstruct this view on which everyone agrees. According to Armstrong, Everett Fox demonstrates that the first sentence can also be read this way:

> At the beginning of God's creating of the heavens and the earth, when the earth was wild and waste [*tohn va-vohu*], darkness over the face of Ocean, breath of God hovering over the face of the waters, God said: Let there be light. (11)

As Karen Armstrong says, "This reading presents a very different view of the creative process. God did not make the world out of nothing, since the waste of chaos and the primal sea were already in existence, and God merely imposed order upon the *tohu va-vohu*" (14).

Four Assumptions

In *The Bible as It Was*, James L. Kugel provides essential background for the project that I am undertaking. Kugel painstakingly demonstrates how exegetes essentially reconstructed the Bible, reconciling contradictions and supplying meanings. For example, Exodus 15:4–5 specifies that the Egyptians sank like stones in the dead sea, but in Exodus 14:30, the Israelites see the dead Egyptians upon the shore. The author of one ancient interpretation (the Wisdom of Solomon) tells us that the bodies first sank to the bottom of the sea and then were cast up on the shore, thus reconciling an apparent contradiction in scripture (16). Furthermore,

> The story of Adam and Eve [. . .] only *became* the story of the Fall of Man thanks to a certain ancient interpretations of one of the verses in the story. The snake in the story came to be identified with the devil—but only by later interpreters, not by the story itself! And it was only because of another interpretation that the Garden of Eden (also known as paradise) came to be thought of as a *heavenly* garden, one in which the righteous would live eternally after their death. (xiv)

The interpretations, which, to a large extent, have become canonical, resulted from four assumptions. First, the Bible is cryptic; as Kugel explains, "[A]lthough Scripture may appear to be saying X, what it really means is Y, or that while Y is not openly said by Scripture, it is somehow implied or hinted at in X" (18). Second, the Bible is a book of instruction, providing guidance for and regulation of life (19). Third, the Bible is perfect and harmonious (20). Fourth, Scripture is divinely inspired (22).

Though Kugel deals with ancient interpretations such as 1 Enoch, parts of which date into the third century BCE, and the Septuagint, a Biblical translation made in stages from the third to the first century BCE, the four assumptions have been constant and guide many current interpreters, particularly fundamentalists, who assume that the lode of meaning lies just beneath the surface of the words on the page, that the Bible is a guide to both spiritual and practical life, that the Bible is a coherent and harmonious totality, and that the Book is the inerrant word of God. Providing explanations of Biblical mysteries, drawing lessons from the Bible, demonstrating the Book's unity, and viewing the Holy Text as the word of God define the projects undertaken by many interpreters.

And the fact of interpretation results from the faith of belief that scripture is determinate: that there is *a* meaning to be found. The eighth of the thirteen Articles of Faith of the Church of Jesus Christ of Latter-Day Saints, delivered by the Prophet Joseph Smith, states,

> We believe the Bible to be the word of God as far as it is translated correctly; we also believe the Book of Mormon to be the word of God.

Mormon doctrine holds that the Book of Mormon is translated correctly and thus is, according to believers who equate accuracy of translation with foundational meaning, determinate, for the work was done under the direct supervision of God, but the caveat about possibly fallacious Biblical translation provides Latter-Day Saints' theology with an escape clause. One must be cautious in reading the Bible, for the original word of God has been corrupted by human fallibility; the Book of Mormon, however, needs no interpretation.

In *Who Speaks for God*, Charles Colson of Watergate fame states his "unyielding commitment to the proposition that neither I, nor anyone else, speaks for God except insofar as they speak founded upon His inerrant word" (13). Yet through the centuries, interpreters have argued about the nature of His inerrant word. In 1997, two articles in *Christianity Today* take diametrically opposed positions regarding Biblical interpretation and translation. One author argues that inclusive-language Bibles, following the fairly recent practice of translating *man* as both *man* and *woman* and using two pronouns (for instance, *he* and *she*), distort scripture (26–32) The answer, from the companion article, is that "The use of inclusive pronouns in translation falls within the realm of dynamic translation theory. In the ancient world it was common to say 'man' or 'he' when speaking of all people" (33–39).

The problems of reaching agreement on *a* meaning of scripture should make interpreters humble and cautious.

Presupposition and Inference

Reading any text is a tradeoff, the reader bringing his or her own knowledge *to* the text (*presupposition*) and thereby deriving new knowledge *from* the text (*inference*).

> Albert, a twenty-nine-year-old college dropout, likes fast cars, expensive clothes, and fine wines. He's marrying a very wealthy seventy-five-year-old woman.

Most readers would *presuppose* that Albert is unmarried since bigamy is not a usual practice, and they would *infer* that Albert is marrying the woman for her money. Neither the presupposition nor the inference is stated in the text; the reader brings the one *to* the text and derives the other *from* the text.

Chapter by chapter, verse by verse, the Bible confronts the careful reader with enigmas, one of which is presented in the following passage.

> Now Eli was very old. He heard all that his sons were doing to all Israel, and how they lay with the women who served at the entrance to the tent of meeting. He said to them, "Why do you do such things? For I hear of your evil dealings from all these people. No, my sons; it is not a good report that I hear the people of the Lord spreading abroad. If one person sins against another, someone can intercede for the sinner with the Lord, but if someone sins against the Lord, who can make intercession?" But they would not listen to the voice of their father; for it was the will of the Lord to kill them. –1 Samuel 2:22–25

Plainly stated, the enigma is this: since the Lord wanted to kill Eli's sons, he made them impervious to the admonitions of their father. Why would the Lord want to kill the sons when their father might have made them repentant? The reader has two choices: first, to ignore the enigma; second, to attempt to rationalize. To make sense of the passage, the reader must construct a rationalization, and the instruments of that construction are presupposition and inference. For example, I might *presuppose* that somehow Eli's sons were evil beyond redemption and thus *infer* that the Lord had reason to slay them.

The Textual Contract

In addition to bringing presuppositions to texts and drawing inferences from texts, readers also come to texts expecting certain norms, which the philosopher Paul Grice has outlined in his book, *Studies in the Ways of Words*. These norms—Grice calls them "the cooperative principle"—are commonsensical and very powerful as we attempt to explain how we try to make sense of language, whether written or spoken. The four components of the cooperative principle are *quality, quantity, manner,* and *relation*. These principles, so apparently simple, yield rich insights when applied to texts as questions or probes. *Quality*: "What is the source? Is the source (he, she, they, it) reliable?" *Quantity*: "Does the text contain all of the material that I need in order to understand it? Does the text contain superfluous material?" *Manner*: "Is the text as clear as it can possibly be in relation to its purpose?" *Relation*: "Do all of the materials in the text relate to that purpose, or are some of the materials unrelated?"

The principle of *quality* is simply this: unless we have reason to believe otherwise, we assume that the writer or speaker is both honest and competent. Everyday experience validates this principle. We do not question the quality of most of the discourse that we encounter: newspaper reports of crime, a physician's diagnosis, directions for assembling new gadgets, and so on. If we are leftwingers, we might not agree with the opinions expressed by George Will in a column, but we do not—or at least I do not—doubt the *quality* of the text. That is, I think that Will is honest and that he knows what he's talking about (though his values may differ from mine).

It is only through the principle of quality that we are able, for instance, to differentiate figurative exaggerations from lies or irony from non-ironic discourse. During his time in Nevada, Mark Twain and a pal hiked up to the pristine Lake Tahoe. In *Roughing It*, he tells us that "Three months of camp life on Lake Tahoe would restore an Egyptian mummy to his pristine vigor, and give him an appetite like an alligator. I do not mean the oldest and driest mummies, of course, but the fresher ones" (158). Because we assume that Mark Twain is not lying and that he is not insane, we take his statements as hyperbole, but we can do so only because we intuitively establish a qualitative norm from which Twain deviates. When Jonathan Swift suggests slaughtering children for food as "A Modest Proposal" for overcoming poverty in Ireland, we know, because of the principle of quality, that his intent is bitter irony and that his "proposal" is deadly serious in its purpose: to shock people into awareness of the dire straits in eighteenth-century Ireland.

The question of Biblical quality is difficult, one of many problems being to establish the most valid text, the version that is nearest to the original. For example, in the address "To the Reader" of the New Revised Standard Version, the editors say, "Occasionally it is evident that the text [of the OT] has suffered in transmission and that none of the versions provides a satisfactory restoration. Here we can only follow the best judgment of competent scholars as to the most probable reconstruction of the original text" (xxvii). In other words, readers often cannot be sure that the text they are reading corresponds with the original (and now lost) text.

The problem of authorship is even more thorny. It was long assumed, for example, that "The Revelation to John" (Apocalypse) was written by the Disciple John, son of Zebedee, an attribution that modern scholarship discredits, the view now being that "Revelation" was composed by an anonymous Jew, "a native of Palestine who emigrated to Asia Minor, perhaps in the wake of the first Jewish revolt against Rome (66–73 CE)" (2307). Traditionally, the Pentateuch is attributed to Moses, but that view is questioned by Biblical scholars, who argue that the first five books of the Bible, and, indeed, the character of Moses, resulted from editors' patching together texts by two different authors, identified, according to their terms for God, as J (who used the term *Jahweh*) and E (who used the term *Elohim*). In other words, much Biblical scholarship leads to the strong probability that there was no historical Moses.

Who, then, is accountable for the Pentateuch? If these books are amalgams, blended by skillful editors, or collages, pasted together by various hands, authenticity comes into question, and the Bible must be viewed, at least in large part, as the work of erring humans.

An easy solution to the problem of Biblical *quality* is simply to attribute authorship to God, divine wisdom guiding the pens of earthly scribes, but like most simple solutions to complex problems, this one merely creates more problems. If the Bible is the word of God, then it is clearly inerrant, and one can take it literally. However, this view brings one to the adamantine wall of historical fact: from about 621 BCE, when the idea of a sacred book of the Hebrews began to take form, until the present day, Christians and Jews have been unable to agree on the "true" form or the "accurate" translation of the Bible. For example, Orthodox, Catholic, and Protestant Bibles differ in significant ways. The Orthodox Bible includes the book of Tobit, which is absent from the Catholic and Protestant Bibles; the Book of Daniel in the Catholic Bible differs from that book in the Protestant Bible, which does not include the Prayer of Azariah, the Song of the Three Jews, or the stories of Susanna and Bel and the Dragon.

At crucial and poignant moments in the Bible, committed readers must be left floundering, wondering what God's intent might really be. For example, compare the following three versions of Matthew 15:4, in which Christ is quoting *Leviticus* 20:9:

> For God commanded, saying, Honour thy faither
> and mother: and, He that curseth father or mother,
> let him die the death.
>
> —*King James Version*

> For God said, 'Honor your father and mother' and 'Anyone who curses his father or mother must be put to death.'
>
> —*New International Version* (1973)

> For God said, 'Honor your father and your mother,' and, 'Whosoever speaks evil of father or mother must surely die.'
>
> —*New Revised Standard Version* (1989)

Here are the passages from Leviticus:

> For every one that curseth his father or his mother shall be surely put to death: he hath cursed his father or his mother; his blood *shall be* upon him.
>
> —*King James*

> If anyone curses his father or mother, he must be put to death. He has cursed his father or his mother, and his blood will be upon his own head.
>
> —*New International*

> All who curse father or mother shall be put to death; having cursed father or mother, their blood is upon them.
>
> —*New Revised Standard*

What, then, was God's intent? In *Leviticus*, all three versions prescribe death for those who curse their parents, but in Matthew, with Christ quoting Hebrew scripture, the *King James* and *New Revised Standard* versions allow us the blessed latitude to interpret the passage as a warning of *spiritual* death for those who commit the mortal sin of filial impiety. I think that this interpretive problem is not trivial in that it is typical rather than extraordinary.

In summary: it seems to me impossible rationally to claim that this or that version or this or that interpretation of scripture is definitive. The principle of *quality* remains an open question, perhaps the single most thorny problem in regard to scripture.

What about *quantity*? Is some content of the Bible superfluous to God's purpose, or does the Bible contain insufficient material for God to achieve His purpose? We know that none of the several versions of the Bible includes all of the texts that have been and that are now available. In fact, when we begin to untangle the snarled concept of the Apocrypha, we see that the principles of *quality, quantity*, and *relation* interact with one another.

Here in outline is the Apocryphal tangle. In the fifth century CE, Saint Jerome coined the term Apocrypha to denote the books that were included in the Greek OT (the Septuagint), but not in the Hebrew Bible. Protestants do not consider these books canonical, and they are either omitted from the King James version or are included only in an appendix.

The books excluded from the Hebrew scriptures were Judith, The Wisdom of Solomon, Tobit, Sirach *(Ecclesiasticus)*, Baruch, the two books of Maccabees, the two books of Esdras, additions to the Book of Esther (10:4–10) , the Song of the Three Young Men (Daniel 3:24–90), Susanna (Daniel 13), Bel and the Dragon (Daniel 14), and the Prayer of Manasseh. However, the Roman Catholic and Orthodox Bibles include all of the Apocrypha except the two books of Esdras and the Prayer of Manasseh.

The raw facts about inclusions and exclusions from versions of the Bible raise questions about quality, quantity, and relation. *Harper's Bible Dictionary* attests to the historical importance of the Apocrypha, but, further, argues that these books "have a potential role in the ecumenical movement as groups of Christians seek for means of communication with one another" (38). Those interested in the Bible, and particularly those who live by it, must ask about the reliability (the *quality*) of the text that they choose, and that question entails the principle of *quantity* ("Is the Aprocrypha necessary for a complete understanding of the Bible?"), which in turn entails the question of *relation* ("Which scriptural materials are relevant and which aren't?"). The questions entailed by the principles of quality, quantity, and relation circle back upon one another, enriching one's inquiry by fusion.

The principle of *manner* entails the problem of the way in which scripture conveys its "truths."

A first example: two versions of Revelation 12:1–2:

> And there appeared a great wonder in heaven; a woman clothed with the sun, and the moon under her feet, and upon her head a crown of twelve stars: ²*And she being with child cried, travailing in birth, and pained to be delivered.*
>
> —*KJ*

> A great portent appeared in heaven: a woman clothed with the sun, with the moon under her feet, and on her head a crown of twelve stars. ²*She was crying out in birth pangs, in the agony of giving birth.*
>
> —*NRSV*

The second verses, which I have italicized, mean essentially the same, but most readers today would find the *NRSV* rendition easier to understand than the *KJ* rendition. The following two sentences are in most ways synonymous, but the second version is much easier to read than the first:

> That Luke claimed that Paul knew that Jesus was holy is true.

> It is true that Luke claimed that Paul knew that Jesus was holy.

In other words, some texts are easier to read than are others, but ease of reading is not necessarily a virtue or strength. A case in point, that I choose virtually at random, is Ecclesiastes 6:7:

> All human toil is for the mouth, yet the appetite is not satisfied.

The meaning of this little adage is not, I presume, immediately apparent for most readers, but when they unpack it, they find a superabundance of ideas and images. First, sensual imagery carries the "message": probably toilers sweating in the sun; the contrasting image of a meal; the evocation of hunger. Second, the allegorical, symbolic value: "human toil" easily translates to all strivings, spiritual and physical; "the mouth" is the receptive "organ," again, whether spiritual or physical; hunger can be satisfied for the moment, but the gnawing returns and always awaits one as one hungers eternally for spiritual sustenance. From the standpoint of the Christian reader, this parable also finds its consummation in the Beatitudes: "Blessed are those who hunger and thirst for righteousness, for they will be filled" (Matthew 5:6).

The last item in the cooperative principle is *relation*: everything in a text will relate to that text's purpose; there will be nothing extraneous.

A corollary of the principle of relation is the fact that readers typically make great efforts to bring coherence to the text. That is, under normal circumstances readers assume that all elements in a text are relevant, if only they can figure out what the relationships are.

Take "The Song of Songs" as a case in point. I well remember when I first read this luscious poetry: during the summer of 1949 for a "Bible as Literature" class at the University of Nevada. I can't recall the professor's explanation of why this work was part of the West's most sacred text, but for an eighteen-year-old such rationalization was beside the point; for me, the poem was erotic, almost as sensational as *This Is My Beloved*, a lurid dithyramb that was circulating around the campus at the time.

If the love portrayed in the Song of Songs is Eros, readers will have difficulty integrating the book into the whole of scripture. What, after all, does profane love, eroticism, have to do with God's message?

Three modern versions of the Bible rationalize the Song of Songs in different ways. The *NIV* places the Song of Songs, with Proverbs, Job, and Ecclesiastes, in the category "wisdom literature." "[I]t is wisdom's description of an amorous relationship. The Bible speaks of both wisdom and love as gifts of God, to be received with gratitude and celebration" (*NIV* 1003). However *NAB* sees the book as allegory. "The Song of Songs, meaning the greatest of songs [. . .] contains in exquisite poetic form the sublime portrayal and praise of the mutual love of the Lord and his people. The Lord is the lover and his people are the beloved." (NAB 791). The *NRSV* is noncommittal, explaining various rationalizations for including the Song of Songs in the Bible. Traditionally, the Jews view the Song as religious allegory of God's love for Israel. "For Christians it is an allegory of Christ's love for the church." And a historical note that perhaps both Christians and Jews would prefer to overlook: the Song is derived "from a ritual marriage between two gods, the fertility god Dummuzi-Tammuz (perhaps represented by the king) and his sister Inanna-Astarte (represented by a priestess)" (*NRSV* 1000).

Karen Armstrong relates one of the strangest attempts to rationalize the Song, making it an integral part of scripture (*History* 214–15). In the *Shiur Qomah* (The Measurement of the Height), a fifth-century text describes God as Ezekiel had seen him on the throne and bases that description on the Song 5:10–15:

> [10]My beloved is all radiant and ruddy,
> distinguished among ten thousand.
> [11]His head is the finest gold;
> his locks are wavy,
> black as a raven.
> [12]His eyes are like doves
> beside springs of water,
> bathed in milk,
> fitly set.

> ¹³His cheeks are like beds of spices,
>   yielding fragrance.
> His lips are lilies,
>   distilling liquid myrrh.
> ¹⁴His arms are rounded gold,
>   set with jewels.
> His body is ivory work,
>   encrusted with sapphires.
> ¹⁵His legs are alabaster columns.

Armstrong tells us that "Some saw this as a description of God: to the consternation of generations of Jews, the *Shiur Qomah* proceeded to measure each one of God's limbs listed here" (*History* 21).

Even Jack Miles, in his brilliant and skeptical *God: A Biography*, is able to integrate the Song. Though, he says, modern historical critics are virtually unanimous in regarding the Song as secular love poetry, "Yet when these poems are read as part of a reading of the Tanakh, they cannot fail to remind us of the only previous love lyrics in the collection—namely, the ardent, if wounded, reconciliation scenes imagined in Isaiah and Hosea" (335).

> For the Lord has called you
> like a wife forsaken and grieved in spirit,
> like the wife of a man's youth when she is cast off,
> says your God.
>
> For a brief moment I abandoned you,
> but with great compassion I will gather you.
> In overflowing wrath for a moment
> I had my face from you,
> but with everlasting love I will have compassion on you,
> says the Lord, your Redeemer.
>   —*Isa. 54:6–8*

> Therefore, I will now allure her,
> and bring her into the wilderness,
> and speak tenderly to her.

> From there I will give her vineyards,
> and make the Valley of Achor a door of hope.
> There she shall respond as in the days of her youth,
> as at the time when she came out of the land of Egypt.
> —*Hos.* 2:14–15

In other words, the Song can be taken by even the most skeptical reader as integral to the OT.

From the standpoint of ethics, the four aspects of the cooperative principle circle back upon themselves, the questions regarding manner inevitably leading to the questions regarding quality, for if the difficulty of a text is unjustified, the author's semantic intention must somehow have been flawed. Perhaps the text was an attempt to bamboozle readers, or perhaps the difficulty resulted merely from carelessness or ignorance. In either case, the writer's ethics come into question.

Ethics: Texts and Readers

One tricky corollary, however, complicates these straightforward principles and the questions that they imply: namely, the concept of *semantic intention*, which transforms the utilitarian "cooperative principle" into an ethical system. Semantic intention is what the author wants the text to *do*. For example, depending on context, the following can be either a threat or a promise: "I assure you that I'll be here tomorrow."

> I'll check to see if you have the work done. *I assure you I'll be here tomorrow.*

> I didn't bring your present today, but *I assure you I'll be here tomorrow.*

Considering semantic intention, readers ask such questions as this: "Is the writer telling the truth, or is he simply trying to con me? Is the text ironic or 'straight'?" Joyce's *Finnegans Wake* is notoriously difficult, perhaps impossible to read if by "reading" we mean deriving the meaning of the whole. The *ethics* of the principle of manner raise this question: was Joyce's semantic intention ethical or unethical? That is, was he attempting to stretch the limits of language and thus open new vistas for readers, or did he construct an elaborate (and monumentally successful) hoax? In the January 1997 issue of *PMLA*, the journal of the Modern Language Association of America, Professor Biddy Martin speaks of the value of "reading that suspends the demand for immediate intelligibility, works at the boundaries of meaning, and yields to the effects of language and imagination" (7). Of course, Martin is dealing not just with the pleasures of reading, but also with the ethics of the language transaction. Should a text go to the very boundaries of meaning? Does an author such as Joyce have the ethical right to demand that readers follow the tortuous path of his text? The answer is, of course, situational. If the writer's semantic intention is to *explain* (how to assemble a new bicycle, how to perform an appendectomy), nothing less than the attempt to achieve ultimate clarity is ethically justified; if the writer's semantic intention is to explore the limits of language or create a new language, the attempt is ethically justified—provided the writer does not present the text as something other than an experiment.

Ethics: Faith and History

I begin with a simple example. Suppose a physician is a devout Christian, believing that prayer brings about cures. *As a physician*, she might prescribe an antibiotic and tell the patient that *some evidence* indicates that prayer facilitates healing (which, I understand, is indeed the case). *As a devout Christian*, not as a physician, she might encourage prayer and might explain her *belief*, based on *faith*, that, through prayer, one gains divine intervention.

In other words, one epistemological system constitutes medicine and quite another constitutes religious faith (and, as I will point out, confusing or conflating any two knowledge or belief systems is disastrous). The Christian doctor would not present a paper at a convention of the American Medical Association arguing, on the sole basis of scripture, that prayer is an agent of healing, nor would she, in a testimonial in a church, claim that medical science proves the intervention of God in human affairs through prayer.

However, I am not concerned with the imprecise science of medicine; rather, I am interested in the fuzzy concept of history. Again, I cook up an example to clarify what I'm getting at. Suppose I say that the holocaust did not happen, but was simply a fabrication of international Judaism (and there are those who make that claim). The common (and commonsensical) response would be that all of the evidence points toward the reality of the holocaust, and every responsible historian verifies the basic claim and the evidence supporting it. In other words, we take the holocaust to be *historical*. It happened, so far as we can determine. However, someone might claim that the holocaust came about because of satanic influences and base this claim on scripture and religious belief systems. Such a claim is *transhistorical*; it does not satisfy the minimal criteria necessary for it to be taken as historical—namely, the claim lacks correspondence (i.e., empirical evidence to back it), and it lacks coherence (i.e., it does not fit into the narrative that tells the story of the Third Reich and the holocaust).

I am not a cynic. In Berchtesgaden, gazing upward toward Kehlsteinhaus, Hitler's "Eagle' Nest," I had a sense of evil and dread; I would not, under any circumstances, have toured the place, for, to me, it emanated an evil that I cannot explain. However, if I used this sense to argue *historically* that Satan empowered Hitler and that evil spirits still inhabited the place, I would have been committing a significant transgression of reasonable and reasoned discourse. ("I can prove that Hitler was under the influence of demonic powers because I felt a sense of evil emanating from Kehlsteinhaus.")

My point, then, is this: the first step on the road to religious madness such as the mass suicide at Jonestown is *transhistoricalism* in regard to scripture and religious beliefs, because the transhistorical allows anyone to explain anything in any way. The disaster arises from the premise that since God can do anything, the myths of religion (and particularly of scripture) are historical narratives. It is worthwhile in this context to remember the Heaven's Gate episode.

The headline and the subhead on the front page of the *Los Angeles Times* for March 28, 1997, read, "39 in Cult Left Recipes of Death. Believed Alien Ship Would Take Them to Heaven. Officials Describe Careful, Ritualistic Suicide. The Dead, Ages 20 to 72, Included 21 Women." They were members of Heaven's Gate,

> which appears to be the successor to a 1970s cult known as the Overcomers or the Human Individual Metamorphosis that flickered in and out of vogue over the last two decades, preaching a philosophy that blends biblical teachings about Jesus with dire warnings about satanic Angels taking over Earth. (Simon, Anderson, and Perry A20)

Their recipe for death was phenobarbital in applesauce or pudding, washed down with vodka. They all had short-cropped hair and wore black, loose-fitting shirts, black trousers, and black Nike shoes. Packed suitcases or flight bags stood ready by the beds on which the cult members died, and many of them carried five dollar bills and rolls of quarters (to pay their toll fees into the other world?). All but two were covered by purple shrouds, over the face and chest.

The suicides apparently took place in three waves. Plastic bags and elastic bands found in the trash behind the house indicated that they had used these for suffocation to speed up demise. Apparently the members of the second wave cleaned up after the first wave, removed the plastic bags, and placed the shrouds. The third wave was two persons, who still had the plastic bags over their heads and were not covered by the purple shrouds.

Authorities found identification in the pockets of most of the dead cultists.

The cultists spoke posthumously through a lengthy letter, a brief video, and various Internet postings. On the video, one thirty-one-year-old woman said,

> "Maybe they're crazy, for all I know. But I don't have any choice but to go for it, because I've been on this planet for 31 years and there's nothing here for me." The group's pending suicide appealed to her, she said, because "if that's what it takes, that's better than being around here with absolutely nothing to do." (A20)

The group also left a video with farewell messages from thirty-eight of the thirty-nine who died. Several talked about their excitement at the prospect of leaving their nine-to-five quotidian and traveling to the "next level." One woman said, "'Everyone in this class wanted something more than the world had to offer'"(A20).

They ran a computer consulting firm called "Higher Source" that, apparently, designed Web pages for Southern California businesses. Interestingly, they apparently rose at 4:00 every morning "to gaze at a star in the northeastern sky that they considered their home."

With regard to any belief system (e.g., the manifest destiny of America, the sanctity of the family, Christ's divinity), it is essential to differentiate the historical and the mythic, else one falls into the trap of transhistoricalism. The Trojan War is generally taken to be historical—that is, based on mountains of evidence, we believe that it actually happened; however, this historicity does not validate *The Iliad*. For example, we cannot argue that since there was a Trojan War, it must be the case that the goddess Athena created Achilles' shield. The historicity of Christ's existence does not establish the historicity of his resurrection. Both the historical fact of Christ's existence and the mythic significance of the resurrection are enormously important for people who read the Bible reverently and critically, but the problems of history and myth belong to separate and largely incompatible knowledge systems. The important question regarding the resurrection is not "Did it happen?" but "What does it mean?"

A great American tragedy resulted from the disjunction between history and faith: the infamous Salem witch trials at the end of the seventeenth century. "Spectral evidence" resulted in the hanging of some twenty people: invisible birds; devils that only certain members of a group of could see; succubi; "shades" of village residents that had simultaneous existence with the corporeal persons and, again, could be perceived only by some. Not all of the evidence against the accused was spectral; there were physical manifestations: witches' teats (deformities of any kind, preferably ones near the pudendum or anus); evil eyes; poppets or dolls, which obviously could be used in conjuring. The magistrates who would hear the witch trials agreed that they would accept as evidence any mischief that resulted after a disagreement between neighbors, and, enlightened as they were, would not perform the water test, which Cotton Mather had condemned as unchristian. "[M]ost important of all, they would accept the doctrine that 'the devil could not assume the shape of an innocent person in doing mischief to mankind'" (Starkey 53).

Related to the transhistorical fallacy (which is my term) is *argument on the basis of ignorance*. Simply because A is unable to disprove B's conclusion does not mean that B's conclusion is valid. Thus, I might argue that the abominable snowman exists because no one has been able to prove that he does not exist. "It is a historical fact that Lot's wife was changed into a pillar of salt because no one has been able to disprove the Biblical story." "Of course the tail of the Hale-Bopp comet conceals a spaceship because no one has been able to prove that such a ship does not exist."

The transhistorical fallacy and argument on the basis of ignorance, both common in religious discourse, are perilous exactly because they create the possibility of Jonestown and Heaven's Gate.

Van A. Harvey has wrestled brilliantly with the problem of history versus faith or faith in the light of history. He says,

> To ask whether an explanation is possible in the practical sense is to ask whether it is a relevant possibility, a likely candidate to account for certain data.[. . .]

> In the case of an alleged miracle, i.e., an event that contradicts our present knowledge in a specific scientific field, like blood raining from heaven, the historian will first ask, "What am I being asked to believe?" and then, "What is to be said in its favor?" It is at this point that present knowledge plays such an important role, for if the report contradicts a well-established warrant, the burden of evidence and argument suddenly falls on the one who alleges the report to be true, which is another way of saying that a *prima facie* case exists for the report *not* being considered a likely candidate. (86–87)

Since a rainfall of blood does not square with either our own experience or with the science of meteorology, the person who reports such a rainfall has a problem, if she wants us to believe, that is. Basing her argument on the omnipotence of God can and, in my experience usually does, lead to nihilism.

Though I make no pretense of being a prophet new inspired, I do have my own solution to the dilemma that comes about when one tries to square faith with history, and I will diffidently offer that solution in a later chapter, but, for the moment, it is enough if I come clean. I agree wholeheartedly with Northrop Frye, who says, "The Bible should be read as literally as any fundamentalist could desire, but the real literal meaning is an imaginative and poetic one" (xv). In my own experience, reading the Bible has been a great imaginative and sublimely poetic experience.

4

Saint Augustine Learns to Read Scripture

> Accordingly, though the obscurity of the divine word has this advantage, that it causes many opinions about the truth to be started and discussed, each reader seeing some fresh meaning in it, yet, whatever is said to be meant by an obscure passage should be either confirmed by the testimony of obvious facts, or should be asserted in other and less ambiguous texts.
>
> —*The City of God* XI.19

I have chosen Saint Augustine of Hippo as my patron saint. His struggles with scripture and his search for a rock upon which to build his citadel of faith are endlessly fascinating and boundlessly heartening. And for me, Augustine's story conveys a moral: the seeker after faith will be the architect and builder of his or her own citadel. Through rationalizing the Biblical enigmas that stymie many seekers, Augustine reached his goal of faith.

We view Augustine standing in all his luminosity on the horizon, behind him the sunset world of Greek and Roman classics and before him the dawning medieval world of Christianity. His conversion is the story of moving from the Latin culture of the late

Roman empire to the Hebraic culture of Holy Scripture. It is the story of Augustine's learning to read the Bible. Augustine's struggles with scripture—richly documented in the *Confessions*, *The City of God*, and *On Christian Doctrine*—are marvelous examples of what happens to the person who seeks to base his or her faith on the Bible.

In his quest for Wisdom, Augustine longs to achieve purity of soul or spirit, rising above the grossness of materiality. And from the standpoint of Scripture, the body is to the spirit as the body of the text is to the Truth therein. Augustine's problem as a reader was to see through the body of text to the truth that this body clothed.

We can begin with Monica, Augustine's mother. *Confessions* gives us vivid images of this remarkable woman. For example, when Augustine decided to leave his position as a teacher in Carthage and better himself in Rome, he deserted his mother, who had followed him to Carthage. As he was about to embark, "She wept bitterly to see me go and followed me to the water's edge, clinging to me with all her strength in the hope that I would either come home or take her with me" (V.8). And this image is particularly apt, for it can symbolize Monica's dilemma and thus be emblematic of Augustine's trek from the fading glory of classical antiquity to the illumination of Medieval Christianity. She had two antithetical wishes for her son: that through the study of Latin rhetoric he become a successful lawyer and that he accept Jesus as the true Messiah, the appointed one of the Father. But the Latin texts of Cicero and the Bible were worlds (and cultures) apart. For an ambitious, highly intelligent rhetorician, the move from one to the other was tortuous. The presuppositions of Latin culture were *not* those of medieval Christianity.

For me, Augustine's journey to faith is archetypical. It is emblematic of the dilemmas, pitfalls, and tentative triumphs that any seeker after faith must experience.

Peter Brown says that Augustine's education was (like my education) "barren" and "frankly pagan" (24), with only four authors studied in detail: Virgil, Cicero, Sallust, and Terence. In the elementary years, Augustine no doubt learned the three R's, inscribing his alphabet on a wax tablet and reciting his numbers "one and one are two, two and two are four," an exercise that he found loathsome, "while the wooden horse and its crew of soldiers, the burning of Troy and even the ghost of Creusa made a most enchanting dream, futile though it was" (*Confessions* I.13).

Considering the pedagogical method of his preceptors, it is not surprising that Augustine did not learn Greek, sine qua non for intellectuals in the late Roman period. "I was constantly subjected to violent threats and cruel punishments to make me learn. This clearly shows that we learn better in a free spirit of curiosity than under fear and compulsion" (*Confessions* I.14).

In grammar school, Augustine learned a method of textual interpretation that is worth thinking about. Students read passages from the classics aloud and expressively, which meant that reading must have been preceded by analysis. The texts of the classics, after all, were inscribed *without gaps between words and without punctuation*; hence, it would have been impossible to read the text extemporaneously. thestudentwouldfirsthavetoseparatewordsandthenphrasesandthensentencesthisisexactlywhattheconventionsofmoderntypographydoforthereaderbutineffectAugustineandhisclassmateshadtodotheirownmentaltypesetting

Two aspects of this literary education must be noted. First, close analysis was preceded by a general understanding of the text. Perhaps an anecdote from my own experience will explain the importance of what I have called " the principle of gross, then close." As a graduate student, I took a semester-long seminar in *Beowulf.* Each week, we were assigned a certain number of lines of the poem and told to be prepared to identify the verse form of each line, the categories of the verbs, and so on. After four months of this close analysis, I realized that I didn't really know what the poem was about even though I had pored over all of the minutiae of form. In other words, reading for understanding must be top-down, not bottom-up.

The reader must gain a general understanding of the text before close analysis begins. This the student in grammar school did.

(How many pastors base their homilies on close readings of Biblical passages out of context?)

Thus, Augustine had a method of reading, which in one sense served him in his struggles with the Bible: he had learned to analyze both the literal and the figurative in Latin texts and thus was ready to cope with the highly figurative narrative of the Bible. On the other hand, he had learned to expect tightly structured texts, quite different from the appositions (the side-by-sidedness) of the Bible.

In *On Christian Doctrine*, Augustine lists the Biblical books that he considers canonical (for in the fifth century CE, the canon was still not completely settled). Then he says,

> In all of these books those fearing God and made meek in piety seek the will of God. And the first rule of this undertaking and labor is, as we have said, to know these books even if they are not understood, at least to read them or to memorize them, or to make them not altogether unfamiliar to us. Then those things which are put openly in them either as precepts for living or as rules for believing are to be studied more diligently and more intelligently, for the more one learns about these things, the more capable of understanding he becomes. (43; II.9)

Thus, indeed, Augustine's study of "grammar" prepared him in this sense both for his struggle with Scripture and for his role as pastor and teacher.

The second noteworthy aspect of the grammatical study is this: the analysis of a text ended with a criticism of both the manner, the author's style, and of matter, the author's ideas. And the manner-matter dichotomy is a crucial duality in the process of Augustine's learning to read scripture. It is an idea to which we will be returning in this discussion.

Compared with the orderliness and coherence of the classical orations in which Augustine had immersed himself, the Bible must have seemed chaotic when he first began his search for wisdom in its pages. For example, the Bible tells the story of Joseph's brothers selling him into slavery (Genesis 37:12–36) and of Joseph's Egyptian captivity and slavery and his reconciliation with his brothers (Genesis 39–50), but the story of Judah and Tamar (Genesis 38) interrupts this narrative and disrupts its coherence. In *The Art of Biblical Narrative*, Robert Alter argues that the juxtaposition of the Tamar story with the Joseph story, constituting an analogy, was "exactly right" for the "implicit theology" of the Bible (12). The point, however, is that Augustine's heritage was the classical Latin tradition, not the heritage of modern literary analysis that Alter brings to his reading.

One reasonable and illuminating way to think about Augustine's conversion is from the standpoint of rhetoric. We can envision the students under the tutelage of a master composing their orations, substituting this word for one more appropriate; rearranging sentences; finding an apt simile for the expression of an idea. We can see them practicing their orations, raising their voices in passion and then almost whispering to force the audience to listen carefully, stamping their feet at appropriate times, and gesturing with clenched fist or open hand. These are the outward manifestations of the rhetoric that Augustine studied.

For the *reader*, the problem would be to dig through the overburden of style and form to find the rich vein of *logos*, the meanings of which include the substance of the text but go beyond that to encompass reason itself, in Greek philosophy the controlling power of the universe, and finally to the divine wisdom that created and governs the universe. Thus, "Word" in the first verse of the Gospel of John might be translated "Divine Wisdom." "In the beginning was the Divine Wisdom, and the Divine Wisdom was with God, and the Divine Wisdom was God."

The rhetorical doctrine that Augustine absorbed, then, implied that style and arrangement could be adjusted to appeal to a given audience without warping the underlying *logos*. And that tradition paradoxically made him resistant to the style of the Bible, yet prepared him to read it for the wisdom it offered regardless of its style and its apparently chaotic arrangement. *Hortensius*, a Ciceronian text that is now lost, was the impetus that started Augustine on his journey toward baptism as a Christian and thus toward sainthood. As a student in Carthage, Augustine ran with other students called the "'Wreckers,' a title of ferocious devilry which the fashionable set chose for themselves" (III.3) He assures us that he had nothing to do with the Wreckers' violence, but felt ashamed of himself because he was not like them.

> These were the companions with whom I studied the art of eloquence at that impressionable age. It was my ambition to be a good speaker, for the unhallowed and inane purpose of gratifying human vanity. The prescribed course of study brought me to a work by an author named Cicero, whose writing nearly everyone admires, if not the spirit of it. The title of the book is *Hortensius* and it recommends the reader to study philosophy. It altered my outlook on life. It changed my prayers to you, O Lord, and provided me with new hopes and aspirations. All my empty dreams suddenly lost their charm and my heart began to throb with a bewildering passion for the wisdom of eternal truth. I began to climb out of the depths to which I had sunk, in order to return to you. For I did not use the book as a whetstone to sharpen my tongue. It was not the style of it but the contents which won me over, and yet the allowance which my mother paid me was supposed to be spent on putting an edge on my tongue. (III.4)

From *Hortensius*, Augustine learned "to love wisdom itself, whatever it might be, and to search for it, pursue it, hold it, and embrace it firmly" (III.4).

The search for wisdom (and, almost certainly, Monica's influence) brought Augustine to the Bible. It is worthwhile to pause and let Augustine speak:

> So I made up my mind to examine the holy Scriptures and see what kind of books they were. I discovered something that was at once beyond the understanding of the proud and hidden from the eyes of children. Its gait was humble, but the heights it reached were sublime. It was enfolded in mysteries, and I was not the kind of man to enter into it or bow my head to follow where it led. But these were not the feelings I had when I first read the Scriptures. To me they seemed quite unworthy of comparison with the stately prose of Cicero, because I had too much conceit to accept their simplicity and not enough insight to penetrate their depths. It is surely true that as the child grows these books grow with him. But I was too proud to call myself a child. I was inflated with self-esteem, which made me think myself a great man. (III.5)

If we view education as indoctrination (which to a certain extent it inevitably is), no conceivable regimen could more thoroughly have prepared Augustine for the cultural shock of reading the Bible: from the calmness, purity, and coherence of Cicero to the turbulence and inconsistencies of scripture. Augustine was caught in the matter-manner dichotomy.

The classical theory of Biblical hermeneutics begins with the *literal* meaning of the text. Thus, for instance, Genesis 1 is taken as the "history" of creation. "Moses wrote these words. He wrote them and then passed on into your presence, leaving this world where you spoke to him" (*Confessions* XI.3). However, "There is a miserable servitude of the spirit in the habit of taking signs for things" (*Doctrine* III.6.84). Thus one can draw a *moral* lesson at every turn and juncture of the Bible.

To receive full value, one must go beyond the moral in Scripture to the *allegorical* meaning. An excellent example is Augustine's Neoplatonic allegorical interpretation of "In the beginning God made heaven and earth."

> "[H]eaven" here means the Heaven of Heavens—that is, the intellectual heaven, where the intellect is privileged to know all at once, not in part only, not as if it were *looking at a confused reflection in a mirror*,[6] but as a whole, clearly, *face to face*;[7] not first one thing and then another, but, as I have said, all at once, quite apart from the ebb and flow of time—and "earth" means the invisible, formless earth, also unaffected by the ebb and flow of time. [. . .] (*Confessions* XII.13)

Finally one reaches the *anagogic* meaning, the mystical content that contains knowledge or hints about the life to come. The last two sections of *The City of God*—"Of the Beatific Vision" and "Of the eternal felicity of the City of God, and of the perpetual Sabbath"—are Augustine's anagogic reading of Scripture.[8]

The levels are not distinctly separate, but often blend into one another. For example, the moral meaning is often derived from an allegorical interpretation, as is the anagogic. In fact, allegory is quite obviously at the heart of any interpretation beyond the literal.

In 384 CE, Augustine was appointed professor of rhetoric in Milan, to teach literature and elocution. There, perhaps for political reasons, he became a catechumen under the auspices of Bishop Ambrose.[9] At first, Augustine admired Ambrose's rhetorical skills of delivery. "So while I paid the closest attention to the words he used, I was quite uninterested in the subject matter and was even contemptuous of it" (*Confessions* V.13). But then came the breakthrough, the epiphany: Augustine realized that the Bible could be, must be, explained figuratively.

> I heard one passage after another in the Old Testament figuratively explained. These passages had been death to me when I took them literally, but once I heard them explained in their spiritual meaning I began to blame myself for my despair, at least in so far as it had led me to suppose that it was quite impossible to counter people who hated and derided the law and the prophets. (*Confessions* V.14)

In fact, literalist interpretation is nothing but "a miserable servitude of the spirit" (*Doctrine* III.6.84), leading one into cul-de-sac after cul-de-sac, unable, for example, to explain shameful acts such as David's lust after Bathsheba and his treachery in sending Uriah, her husband, to his death on a forlorn military hope (*Doctrine* III.12–22.90–98).

But now Augustine traps himself in a paradox. The Bible is "hard indeed to fathom" (*Confessions* XII.10), yet the message is available to any reader. (St. Anthony, though illiterate, memorized the Sacred Scriptures simply by hearing them, and "understood them through prudent thinking" (*Doctrine* "Prologue," 4)). Typically, Augustine hedges his bet, saying that Scripture has layers of meaning, and that anyone can gain the more superficial. For example, the Bible says "the earth was invisible and without form, and darkness reigned over the deep." The sentence is "so worded as to be intelligible in some degree to people who are unable to conceive of utter absence of form" (*Confessions* XII.12).

Which leads us to the ultimate question: Is the Bible determinate? Do the words of Scripture convey A Truth? Is A Truth to be discovered in Scripture? How could Augustine's answer be anything but "yes"? And yet? And yet? People of good will *do* offer various interpretations; people of good will *do* differ about meanings of Scripture. Augustine must rationalize:

> How can it harm me if I understand the writer's meaning in a different sense from that in which another understands it? All of us who read his words do our best to discover and understand what he had in mind, and since we believe that he wrote the truth, we are not so rash as to suppose that he wrote anything which we know or think to be false. Provided, therefore, that each of us tries as best he can to understand in the Holy Scriptures what the writer meant by them, what harm is there if a reader believes what you, The Light of all truthful minds, show him to be the true meaning? It

> may not even be the meaning which the writer had in mind, and yet he too saw in them a true meaning, different though it may have been from this. (*Confessions* XII.18)

Here Augustine seems to be making a desperate attempt, a poignant effort, to reconcile disparate interpretations and thus preserve Biblical determinacy: The One Truth. God will guide the sincere reader who really seeks the truth. In effect, however, Augustine is virtually and inadvertently Nietzschean, denying that A Truth can be found.

> How wonderful are your Scriptures! How profound! We see their surface and it attracts us like children. And yet, O my God, their depth is stupendous. We shudder to peer deep into them, for they inspire in us both the awe of reverence and the thrill of love" (*Confessions* XII.14).

How could it be otherwise, given the mysteries that Scripture unveils to the fit reader?

One might say, as I *do* say, that the cooperative principle is a modern summary of Augustine's theory about the integrity of the Bible. The believer must come to it with complete trust in its truthfulness (quality); its adequacy to convey that truth (quantity); its coherence and unity (relation); and its relative clarity (manner), considering the difficulty of the ideas being conveyed. We can say, for Augustine, that all serious readers of Scripture are governed by the maxims of the cooperative principle. Thus, it is completely understandable that readers can be sincere and diligent, yet differ in their interpretations. Readers bring their own presuppositions and world knowledge to texts; thus, from texts they construct their own meanings, which may or may not agree with a community of interpreters. They supply bridging assumptions, and their inferences can be wildly divergent. Yet they are sincere!

That, of course, leaves Augustine in the dilemma of indeterminacy where there is no final Truth, and he sensed the dilemma and tried to solve it through a metaphor. Some readers "despise the words of Scripture as language fit for simpletons" and fall out of the nest where they were reared (*Confessions* XII.27).

> But there are others for whom the words of Scripture are no longer a nest but a leafy orchard, where they see the hidden fruit. They fly about it in joy, breaking into song as they gaze at the fruit and feed upon it. For when they read or hear these words, they see that you endure, constant and unchanging, supreme above all past or future time, and yet there is no temporal creature that was not of your making. (*Confessions* XII.28)

In other words, finally, all readings are anagogic and lead to the same Truth: the constant and unchanging God behind the words of the text.

5

Sin and Guilt

> . . . what in me is dark
> Illumine, what is low raise and support;
> That, to the height of this great argument,
> I may assert Eternal Providence,
> And justify the ways of God to men.
>
> —Milton, *Paradise Lost*

> Know then thyself, presume not God to scan;
> The proper study of Mankind is Man.
>
> —Pope, *Essay on Man*

He was the most inept of students—a young man who was completely out of place in a freshman English class in a large state university. In a paper about wolverines, he wrote, "The wolverian is a corss bitwin a beer and a snuck," which, translated, means, "The wolverine is a cross between a bear and a skunk," the intention of which was to say that the wolverine *looks like* a cross between a bear and a skunk. At the very beginning of my career, this unfortunate young man was my student, I a teaching assistant working on a doctorate. For the faculty in the English department, both graduate teaching assistants and regular professors, this sentence became the sign and evidence of the decline of literacy in the population and of the decline of standards in the university. Though mercifully he was unaware of it, the student became an object of guffaws and scorn, a symbol of the stupidity and cultural barbarism of the unanointed.

In my relationships with this student, I was never bluntly brutal, but he must have sensed my scorn, and I made no attempt to help him survive the trauma of being on an alien planet surrounded by robotic creatures of whom he would ultimately be the victim. I was in my red-pencil phase, splattering my students' papers with the scarlet letters (Frag, CF, Par, Sp[10]) branding the students' illiteracy. I have no exact memory of what I said about "A wolverian is a corss bitwin a beer and a snuck," but I'm certain the comment was biting and witty. I'm equally certain that my comment and my whole attitude toward this student must either have devastated him or have contributed to his growing anger and frustration.

It was years until this episode in my long career brought the onus of guilt and remorse to me. Far too late, I have come deeply to regret what I did to this student. Far too late, I have come deeply to regret the evils that I caused those who associated with me and those I loved.

Not that I am an extraordinarily sinful person. I represent the everyday, ordinary sinner. In the sum total of things—in a universe that contained the Holocaust—my sins are small potatoes, but my view is not universal, my focus being sharply on my own past, both remote and recent. Many of the acts that tradition would call sinful bother me not in the least: lechery here and mendacity there, periods of sloth, episodes of gluttony, and perpetual green-eyed envy soured into personal enmity expressed by semi-conscious mutterings. I use myself for a case study in the nature of quotidian sinfulness.

The wages of sin is guilt. My sense of guilt causes me to suffer, but this spiritual discomfort, becoming, at times, almost an agony, is, paradoxically, a blessing, allowing me to sense a cleansing of my soul, giving me penance for my sins.

I ask myself, "Am I entitled to such a facile easing of my conscience?" Of late, I am much given to requiems, those of Brahms, Fauré, Mozart, and Verdi and to the eerie insistence of Philip Glass and the mysticism of Hovhaness. As I listen, I mull over the injustices I have done my wife, the traumas I have caused students, my intolerance of my disturbed and disturbing mother. But the catalogue of my sins is really beside the point. What interests me is the relationship between the evil I have done and my sense of guilt for that evil. What interests me is what I take to be the universal phenomenon of evil and guilt.

An acquaintance told me the other day that at the end of the services each Sunday, the priest implores the congregants to pray for forgiveness of their sins. "But," says my Christian friend blandly, "I can't think of anything to ask forgiveness for." Which of us is pathological, my sinless friend or guilt-ridden I? What credit can I take for the esthetically satisfying expiation of my own guilt? What I do know is that I have deep regrets. Perhaps that is enough to humanize me.

The greatest problem of theology must be to develop the perfect theodicy—in other words to reconcile God's benevolence and omnipotence with the problem of evil.

1. Evil exists.

2. God is benevolent.

3. God is omnipotent.

To eliminate the first premise is to deny that evil exists. To eliminate the second premise is to deny God's benevolence. To eliminate the third premise is to deny God's omnipotence.

The easiest solution to the problem is that of Leibniz, who argued that ultimately a transcendent "calculus" would enable us to understand God's universe and the reason for evil in it, for this is, after all, the best of all possible worlds; though we humans are benighted, ultimately the light will dawn.

At the other extreme, in the darkness where I find myself, is Nietzsche, who tells us that the reality which *Is* and the *Ought* which is the ideal cannot be reconciled. One always condemns the other. But perversely, in the attempt to reconcile Is and Ought, we invent God and torture ourselves with the chimera of what-might-be: if only we had the prescience, all of life's tragedy would make sense, as if anyone could translate the meaninglessness of life into a meaningful narrative or a coherent statement.

In the prelapsarian world, there were no earthquakes, tornadoes, plagues, or erupting volcanoes; these evils, traditional theology tells us, resulted from Adam's fault and fall. Until the Enlightenment, the clergy and laity took natural disasters to be evils inflicted on humankind by an omnipotent deity. As John Donne said, "Moving of the earth brings harms and fears. Men reckon what it did and meant." With Rousseau, according to Susan Neiman, the idea that natural disasters were God's punishment for sinfulness was supplanted by a "modern" vision of nature's forces at work having nothing to do with human sinfulness. "Natural disaster" replaced "Natural Evil."

I, however, adapt the concept of Natural Evil for my own purposes. There are the monsters who by *nature* commit evil acts. I knew such a person, a hydrocephalic, mentally defective child who bashed puppies to death and who attempted to smother his baby sister. This child, of course, was incapable of feeling guilt and hence was not guilty. If a person is *naturally* incapable of *feeling* guilt, can he or she sin? Is a mass murderer such as William Bonin or Jeffrey Dahmer a sinner if that person has no sense of guilt—that is, in common parlance, has no conscience? Of course, both Bonin and Dahmer were unquestionably guilty in the legal sense as defined by the McNaghten rule: both knew the "nature and quality" of their actions and that what they did was wrong (according to law and community standards). Bonin, "the Freeway Killer," had murdered and sexually mutilated twenty-one boys and men, yet he expressed no remorse and uncannily seemed detached from his own fate as he awaited execution by lethal injection. The *Los Angeles Times* of February 24, 1966, describes his last hours thus:

> Bonin, who spent his final hours watching the television show "Jeopardy," eating pizza and ice cream and chatting with a Catholic prison chaplain, was moved from his death-watch cell just before midnight. He did not struggle, walking himself to the

> table where he would die. Technicians had trouble finding a good vein, and accidentally punctured a usable vein in his left arm and had to start over, said prison spokesman Vernell Crittendon.

From all indications, there was a void in Bonin's personality, a blank spot in his mind and soul, a mis-wiring in his brain, a genetic defect—something uncanny and beyond the realm in which "conscience" is operative, in which the sense of guilt is activated. Bonin apparently could not feel sorry even for himself.

As *reasonable* men, Bonin and Dahmer knew what they did was wrong, but as *natural* men, they were clearly members of that class termed "psychopath" by some and "sociopath" by others, deviance that Robert D. Hare characterizes in *Without Conscience*. They were glib and superficial, egocentric and grandiose; they lacked remorse or a sense of guilt and empathy; they were deceitful and manipulative and shallow emotionally. They were impulsive, could not control their behavior, needed excitement, lacked responsibility, had behavior problems early in life, and were antisocial (Hare 34).

Neiman (90–91) cites an anecdote from Kant's *Critique of Practical Reason* that is salient here. A man must enter and patronize whenever he passes a brothel. His desire seems uncontrollable. But if this sex fiend were to be shown a gallows on which he would be hanged immediately after he had satisfied his desire, he would, according to Kant, be quite able to resist his urges. To Kant's argument, one codicil must be added: *if the patron of whores were naturally evil, the gallows would be no deterrent*. Or we can go to de Sade's *argumentum ad absurdum*. Since all crimes are natural, there can be no such thing as a crime against nature. In *Dialogue between a Priest and a Dying Man*, the priest asks the dying man to repent. But, says the dying man, I have repented according to my own interpretation of what repentance means.

> By Nature created, created with very keen tastes, with very strong passions; placed on this earth for the sole purpose of yielding to them and satisfying them, and these effects of my creation being

naught but necessities directly relating to Nature's fundamental designs, or, if you prefer, naught but essential derivatives proceeding from her intentions in my regard, all in accordance with her laws, I repent not having acknowledged her omnipotence as fully as I might have done, I am only sorry for the modest use I made of the faculties (criminal in your view, perfectly ordinary in mine) she gave me to serve her; I did sometimes resist her, I repent it. (165–66)

It greatly interests me that in my own acts I have had much in common with Bonin and the hydrocephalic idiot. On occasion, evil has been as natural to me as breathing. In my deplorable reaction to the student who wrote about "wolverians," and in my relationship with him, I was simply doing what came naturally in my role as an acolyte intellectual, humanist, and scholar. My goal in life was to join that rarefied priesthood of those who professed literature and thus, presumably, dispensed sweetness and light, but whose culture valued cleverness and cynicism. In my actions, I was doing what comes naturally in a corrupt culture.

However, there is more to the story than that. In my actions and in my values, I was not atypical of the witty, cynical aspiring neophyte scholars and well ensconced professors surrounding me. Yet now I realize that there was something more: a kind of sociopathic lack of empathy that kept me from identifying with the agonies of others, that insulated me from emotional reactions to tragedies large and small. At the time, my wife, my dear wife, was suffering hellishly with clinical depression, and this in the age before Prozak, Zoloft, and Celexa. All this courageous woman could hope for was alleviation of her misery through "the talking cure" and the *empathetic* sympathy of a loving family. As I look back, I realize that Norma's suffering fazed me very little, engaged as I was in defense of my own ego and in the struggle to become a member of the intellectual elite who dispense sweetness and light in the academy. I was too shallow emotionally to identify with and understand either my wife or my student. I was, I think, incapable of love.

The blessing that maturity and old age have conferred on me is the ability to be empathetic, to identify, and to love. And to regret my past.

I suppose there is a touch of natural evil in all of us, but my concern is not with the Bonins or the Dahmers. I am interested in what I might call "everyday evil," perpetrated by you and me and everyone else—except Christ and, apparently, my church-going, Christian friend.

What I call "routine evil" comes about from those who are simply doing their jobs within institutions. A good example is Albert Speer, who was the epitome of routine evil, Hitler having promoted him from official architect of the Third Reich to armaments minister in charge of providing materiel for war. Speer functioned with admirable skill; he was the ideal administrator, perfectly satisfied as long as he was doing his job—and I think that "job," not "duty," is the right term here, for Speer was singularly without convictions. In fact, Speer shielded himself from direct knowledge of or involvement in the Final Solution. On one occasion Nazi party functionary Karl Hanke mentioned a camp in Upper Silesia, which must have been Auschwitz. In his book *The Third Reich*, Speer said, "I did not want to know what was happening there [. . .] for fear of discovering something that would make me turn from my course" (qtd. in Fest 189).

The perfect example of a routinely evil person is Adolf Eichmann, the subject of Hannah Arendt's classic study. He was a creature of the quotidian, an everyday family man, and in terms of the Third Reich, he was perfectly normal, a law-abiding citizen. In a study that, because of the horrors it documents, is difficult to read, Daniel Jonah Goldhagen portrays such Third Reich monsters as Karl Wagner of the SS unit in charge of a "work camp" at Majdanek, who forced female prisoners to undress before he beat them to death with a whip (Goldhagen 307). Even as you and I, Wagner would have disgusted Eichmann. When forced directly to observe a mass killing, Eichmann was nauseated and horrified. "I hardly looked; I could not; I could not; I had had enough" (qtd. in Arendt 87). He was a man of conscience, who, he said, lived by the ethic of Kant's categorical imperative, "Act only according to that maxim by which you can at the same time will that it should become a universal law," which, in the Third Reich, had, as Arendt (136) points out, been transformed into "Act in such a way that the Führer, if he knew your action, would approve it." And Eichmann could find no one who disapproved of the Final Solution (Arendt 116). Why should he hold himself accountable for acts that were universally approved? It is a stunning irony that Eichmann considered himself a Pontius Pilate. Reflecting back on the Wannsee Conference, when the Nazi hierarchy actually began to map out the Final Solution, Eichmann said, "At that moment, I sensed a kind of Pontius Pilate feeling, for I felt free of all guilt." What had he to feel guilty about when "the most important people had spoken, the Popes of the Third Reich"? (qtd. in Arendt 114). The Pharisees had ordered the mass crucifixion, enabling Eichmann, like Pilate, to wash his hands of the whole affair and let matters take their course.

So this everyday man of conscience went about his duties methodically and assiduously. He kept track of the capacities at the various camps and arranged transport to the camps from the sites where Jews had been assembled by the SS and other units of the Nazi terror. Eichmann was routinely—and *greatly*—evil.

In what sense was the evil I perpetrated in the case of the "Wolverian" student simply routine? Was I an Albert Speer, merely doing my job? The complete answers to these questions would take us on a multi-page aside, the gist of which can be stated thus: during the first years of my career, the academy made no provision for students who needed special help or who should have been counseled out of higher education and into more suitable paths toward their futures. The practice, if not the stated philosophy, was Darwinian, survival of the fittest, and the fittest were, by and large, the economically and socially privileged. Like Speer, I was doing my job in a corrupt system. My evil was routine.

Beyond routine, there is an evil that I call "diabolical." The diabolically evil person creates the situation or system in which routine evil can flourish.

The prime example of *diabolical* evil is Hitler, yet somehow Himmler is more sinister. Hitler's diabolism was eerily disinterested. There are no records of Hitler's having visited the death camps to watch the agonies of the dying; one envisions him above it all, in his alpine Eagle's Nest, boring guests with his interminable monologues and then bursting into one of his rants against the Jew conspiracy to humble the Vaterland. As Ian Kershaw convincingly argues in his massive biography of Hitler, der Führer ranted out his ideology, but remained aloof from its implementation. As Kershaw says, Hitler was "at one and the same time the absolutely indispensable fulcrum of the entire regime, and yet largely detached from any formal machinery of government" (*Hitler: 1889–1936 Hubris* 532). In following Hitler's will, not his direct orders, Nazi functionaries set up the machinery of the Holocaust. Hitler was Milton's Satan.

On the other hand, Himmler was a sadist, delighting in Schadenfreude. He was not the disinterested, dispassionate bureaucrat carrying out the orders of his Fuehrer. On the contrary, he was the architect of the Final Solution, and he morbidly viewed the horrors of the death camps..

Visiting Minsk in 1941, Himmler told the commander of the Einsatzgruppe, Arthur Nebe, that he wanted to view an execution. Nebe rounded up two hundred or so alleged partisans and marched them outside the city to the area of a deep trench. Group after group, the victims were ordered to lie face down in the trench, and the policemen under Nebe's command shot them. After one group had been executed, the bodies were covered with a shallow layer of earth, and another group, forced to lie atop the bodies of their fellow victims, were shot.

Quite understandably, the executioners became more and more disquieted, but Himmler assured them that they were simply doing their duty and that the responsibility was his, not theirs (Breitman 195–96).

Himmler took more than an administrative and bureaucratic interest in the extermination camps. In 1941, he visited the deadly Mauthausen camp and viewed abuse of prisoners so brutal that many committed suicide (Breitman 161).

The aloof, disinterested diabolism of Hitler. The sadistic diabolism of Himmler. The diabolical Winterowd?

Insofar as I was architect of the class (a sub-system of a sub-system) in which the *naturally* and *routinely* evil act of my relationship with the Wolverian student was the norm and not a one-time anomaly, then I was diabolically evil, for I created and perpetuated the system whereby a group of beings suffered. (In my own defense, I must say that throughout my career, I have had largely favorable evaluations by my students, and even the least favorable did not compare my classes to Auschwitz or me to Commandant Höss.)

On the basis of my argument, I make what is perhaps a grandiose claim. I believe that my rubric of evil—natural, routine, and diabolical—enables one to gain insight into evils committed against one, around one, and by one.

But my rubric is incomplete, for I do not include *sins of the body*. As long as a pure soul is trapped in a corrupt body, sin and hence guilt are inevitable. After he found faith, the dilemma of a sinful body clothing a pure soul troubled Augustine constantly and deeply.

6

Augustine's Sin

> As a youth I had been woefully at fault, particularly in early adolescence. I had prayed to you for chastity and said, "Give me chastity and continence, but not yet." For I was afraid that you would answer my prayer at once and cure me too soon of the disease of lust, which I wanted satisfied, not quelled.
>
> —*Confessions*

In his odyssey toward the Ithaca of faith and wisdom, Augustine paused for almost a decade at Manichaeism, a dualistic gnosticism in which spirit was holy and body corrupt. In many ways, the classical, dualistic rhetoric that had formed Augustine prepared him for the dualism of Manichaeism: spirit can equate with *logos*, the meaning of the text, while body is the equivalent of the style in which the text is written.

Founded in Persia in the third century CE by Mani, the "Apostle of Light," Manichaeism was a gnostic sect that offered salvation to believers through special knowledge (*gnosis*) of spiritual truth. For the Manichaean, the soul, which partakes of God, is trapped in the corruption of flesh, a bondage to be overcome only through arcane wisdom such as that found in Mani's revelations. After death, the corrupt body returns to the dust, but the souls of those who persist in fleshly pleasures (e.g., sexual intercourse, eating meat, drinking wine) are recycled through another body while pure souls are reunited with God.

Two aspects of the Manichaean version of gnosticism are important: the inward, personal nature of the gnosis through which salvation was gained and the doctrine of two gods, one malevolent and the other benevolent.

The secret knowledge of gnosticism is revealed to the elect without the intervention of media, as if God had imprinted the message on the mind and soul of the seeker. Therefore, the search for Truth is introspective and, hence, creative, with the result that gnosticism generated libraries of mystic literature, some of it extremely powerful.

Though Manichaean theology is not consistent, and in fact varies according to the inspiration of the author, it posits dual gods, one the spirit of light and the other the darkness of material being. The dark god is the creator of the physical cosmos and of humankind, the sorry race in which spirit is trapped in the corruption of flesh. As Augustine put it in *Confessions*, "Bodily desire, like a morass, and adolescent sex welling up within me exuded mists which clouded over and obscured my heart [. . .]" (II.2).

Throughout his long life, Augustine struggled with the paradox of a soul imprisoned in a willful and sinful body. The true and profound meaning of the Bible is imprisoned in a willful text.

Augustine's struggle with his own bodily desires is a perfect analogy to his movement from style to pure meaning (*logos*). *The City of God* XIV.23 is a treatise on the penis and its incorrigibility: "Whether generation should have taken place even in Paradise had man not sinned, or whether there should have been any contention between chastity and lust." Before the fall, Adam, through his will, could control his penis as he did his limbs, but after the fall "culpable disobedience" brought the curse of "penal disobedience." In XIV.24, he continues obsessively: "[I]f men had remained innocent and obedient in Paradise, the generative organs should have been in subjection to the will as the other members are." Here is Augustine at his eccentric, obsessive best:

> There are persons who can move their ears either one at a time or both together. [. . .] Some, by lightly pressing their stomach, bring up an incredible quantity and variety of things they have swallowed, and produce whatever they please, quite whole, as out of a bag. [. . .] Some have such command of their bowels, that they can break wind continuously at pleasure, so as to produce the effect of singing. (*City* XIV.24; 473)

Before the fall, Adam had been able to control his penis for its proper function, the generation of offspring. In "the new spiritual body into which the flesh of the saints shall be transformed," "the deformity of our penal condition" will be rectified (XXII.21). In the resurrection, "the female members shall remain adapted not to the old uses, but to a new beauty which, far from provoking lust, now extinct, shall excite praise to the wisdom and clemency of God [. . .]" (XXII.17).

Ultimately, Augustine will mortify the flesh, saying that any pleasure other than the spiritual is corrupt, even eating and drinking (*Confessions* X.31). Things of the flesh are not to be enjoyed for themselves, but are to be used as means to the only real pleasure, the love of God (*Doctrine* I.24).

However, Augustine was never completely satisfied with Manichaeism. For one thing, it led to the Marcionite heresy, positing the existence of an evil angelic spirit—Satan—equal in power and knowledge to the Light, or God. So to controvert the Manichaean tenet that powers of darkness (i.e., of matter) created evil, Augustine follows the dialectic of Nebridius, his friend from youth who converted to Christianity with him in Italy and died in Thagaste in 390 CE. If asked about these powers of darkness and the answer were that they could harm God, the Manichaean would have been saying that God is subject to corruption. If, on the other hand, the Manichaean said that the dark powers could not harm God, there would be no point in speaking of the battle between good and evil.

> Therefore, whatever you are—that is, whatever the substance by which you [God] are what you are—if they admitted that you were incorruptible, all their theories were proved to be false and repugnant. If they said you are corruptible, it would be an obvious falsehood, no sooner uttered than rejected in horror. (*Confess* VII.2)

Ultimately, Augustine will come to an analogous conclusion regarding Scripture. It is an obvious falsehood to claim that Scripture is corruptible through its style, its eloquence.

Neoplatonism was the viaticum by means of which Augustine at last reached Ithaca, his odyssey ended.

Augustine's version (his distillation[11]) of Neoplatonism is both apposite and clear. At the lowest level of being are the *senses*: smell, touch, taste, and so on. The *soul*, which might be termed mere awareness, apprehends the facts of sense, and both humans and animals have this awareness. What separates beasts from humans is *reason*, the ability to judge and arrange the brute facts supplied to the perceiving soul by the senses. Beyond reason or intellect is the eternal, immutable *Truth* (*Confessions* VII.17). Thus, Augustine arrives at the most decisive and sublime moment of his quest:

> This power of reason, realizing that in me too it was liable to change, led me on to consider the source of its own understanding. It withdrew my thoughts from their normal course and drew back from the confusion of images which pressed upon it, so that it might discover what light it was that had been shed upon it when it proclaimed for certain that what was immutable was better than that which was not, and how it had come to know the immutable itself. For unless, by some means, it had known the immutable, it could not possibly have been certain that it was preferable to the mutable. And so, in an instant of awe, my mind attained to the sight of God who IS. Then, at last, *I caught sight*

> *of your invisible nature, as it is known through your creatures.* (*Confesionss* VII.17)

From Augustine's point of view, the Pauline epistles were totally in accord with Neoplatonism.

> So I seized eagerly upon the venerable writings inspired by your Holy Spirit, especially those of the Apostle Paul. [. . .] I began to read and discovered that whatever truth I had found in the Platonists was set down here as well, and with it there was praise for your grace bestowed. (*Confessions* VII.21)

Paul was a speaker of Greek and thus, as an educated man, could not have missed the overlay of Platonism in Greek thought. Regardless, however, of Platonic influence on Paul, his theology and Augustine's Platonism were concordant. Though our outer nature wastes away, says Paul, "We look not at what can be seen but at what cannot be seen; for what can be seen is temporary, but what cannot be seen is eternal" (2 Cor 4:16).

Throughout his long life, sexual desire—the original sin, the body's resistance to the dictates of will—tormented Augustine. In 413, at the age of 59, Augustine began work on *The City of God*, a project that he finished only thirteen years later, at the age of 72. Toward the middle of this work, in Book XIV, Augustine descants on "the evil of lust—a word which, though applicable to many vices, is specially appropriated to sexual uncleanness" (XIV.16; 464). If only, he says, it were possible to beget children without lust, controlling "the members created for this purpose" as one controls the other members, through volition. But even those who delight in sex, whether lawful or transgressive, are not in control; their acts are not dictated by their wills. And then the old man's lament, in this pre-Viagra age:

> [B]ut sometimes this lust importunes them in spite of themselves, and sometimes fails them when they desire to feel it, so that though lust rages in the mind, it stirs not in the body. (XIV.16; 464–5)

The spirit that longed to achieve "the universal peace which the law of nature preserves through all disturbances" (*City* XIX.13; 690) was still trapped in the turbulence of bodily desires.

7

The Bible: The Enigmas

> Then one of the seraphs flew to me. . . . And he
> said, "Go and say to this people:
> 'Keep listening, but do not comprehend;
> Keep looking, but do not understand.'
>
> —*Isaiah 6*

I have said that prayer has failed me, or perhaps I have failed prayer, and the Bible leaves me equally unsatisfied. For believers, the Bible is, as it was for Saint Augustine, a source not only of wisdom and beauty, but of Truth. For me, the Bible is a source of wisdom and beauty, but not of truth. Why do millions and millions find answers to their search for faith in the Bible while I find only mystery?

In *The Signifying Monkey*, Henry Louis Gates, Jr., explains a wonderful Yoruba myth,[12] which, in my own "translation," goes like this: Ifa is the god of truth, of what we might call determinate meaning. For Ifa, a text—the Bible, the Constitution, *War and Peace*—has one meaning; the text is determinate. However, our only access to this true meaning, to this truth, is through Esu, and he is a trickster. Thus, we request that Esu find from Ifa the "true" meaning of, say, the Book of Job, and Esu brings us an answer that, paradoxically, we cannot trust, for we know that Esu is unreliable and that he has a perverse sense of humor. In fact (and this is my extension of the myth), we have only Esu's assurance that Ifa actually exists; we cannot be certain. We are left with the agony of doubt regarding those texts that mean the most to us, that we consider most valuable.

This myth memorably captures the dilemma of every reader grappling with a text such as the Bible, the Koran, or *The Book of Mormon*. Between us as readers and the truth we seek stands the enigmatic text, and we cannot trust the meaning that we derive therefrom. It is this dilemma that I want to discuss.

An anatomy of reading is a chart of the reader's intellect, values, attitudes, limitations, predilections, prejudices—of the reader's mind and (dare I say it?) soul. In a sense, then, this chapter is a chart of my mind and (dare I say it?) soul.

Some of the enigmas of the Bible are not so enigmatic when one thinks about them. Here is a case in point: After the crucifixion, and after Mary Magdalene had found the tomb empty, the disciples had assembled,

> . . . and the doors of the house where the disciples had met were locked for fear of the Jews. . . .

Tradition as well as the four gospels allow us to assume that the Jews would persecute Christ's followers; indeed, tradition makes such a presupposition virtually inevitable. However. . . . I remember vividly when I realized the implications of this passage. It was an Easter service, and the minister was delivering a message based on the account of the crucifixion and resurrection. It dawned on me that something here was badly amiss.

Suppose a modern history had said, "Martin Luther King locked the doors of his house for fear of the Americans." After all, Martin Luther King was an American, and his fear was not of Americans in general, but of a kind of American, a subset of the category Americans such as the Klan. Since Christ and his disciples were Jews, since they considered themselves Jews, and since they believed that Christ was the Jewish Messiah, the passage from the Gospel of John becomes problematic, and the automatic presupposition of readers comes into question. The passage makes sense only if it was written retrospectively, after Christianity as a sect began to develop. At the time of the crucifixion there was no Christianity. In fact, scholarly sources date the Gospel of John no earlier than about 80 CE.[13] Thus, the ideological structure built on a common presupposition crumbles: it is most unlikely that the author of the Gospel was John, son of Zebedee and one of Jesus's disciples.

I frequently hear ministers and laypeople say that God's word through the Bible is perfectly clear; Scripture offers answers to all questions and provides an outline for the moral life. Yet when I read the Bible, and think about it, I find its power is precisely its open-endedness; from my point of view, it is what is often called an open or "writerly" text, not giving the reader certainty and determinateness.

One case in point is the Bible's teachings about homosexuality. Leviticus 20:13 is perfectly clear; those who commit homosexual acts must be put to death:

> If a man lies with a male as with a woman, both of them have committed an abomination; they shall be put to death; their blood is upon them.

In fact, the God in Leviticus 20:1–21 is radically conservative in his views of the death penalty. Leviticus specifies capital punishment for the following crimes: turning to mediums and wizards; cursing one's father and mother; committing adultery with the wife of one's neighbor, with one's father's wife, or with one's daughter-in-law; taking both a wife and a mother (death by burning); sex with an animal. (Even anti-death penalty radicals might agree on one pronouncement: that those who sacrifice their children to Moloch deserve to be executed.)

In the Old Testament homosexuality is mentioned only twice, though not by that name (Leviticus 18:22, 20:13), but there are other hints and allusions. For example, Deuteronomy 22:5 condemns cross-dressing:

> A woman shall not wear a man's apparel, nor shall a man put on a woman's garment; for whoever does such things is abhorrent to the Lord your God.

The authors of the Old Testament were, of course, preoccupied with genitals, not only in the ritual use of circumcision, but in strange manifestations such as these:

> No one whose testicles are crushed or whose penis is cut off shall be admitted to the assembly of the Lord. (Deut 23:1)

> If men get into a fight with one another, and the wife of one intervenes to rescue her husband from the grip of his opponent by reaching out and seizing his genitals, you shall cut off her hand; show no pity. (Deut 25:11)

When one begins to think about Leviticus 20:13 in the context of other Biblical pronouncements and narratives regarding sex and homosexuality, the straightforward clarity of the matter starts to grow murky, like pond water when the silty bottom is stirred.

What can one make, for instance, of Genesis 19:1–11 and Judges 19:22–26, in which virgin daughters are sacrificed in order to save men from homosexual rape? Here is the passage from Judges:

> While they were enjoying themselves, the men of the city, a perverse lot, surrounded the house, and started pounding on the door. They said to the old man, the master of the house, "Bring out the man who came into your house, so that we may have intercourse with him." And the man, the master of the house, went out to them and said to them, "No, my brothers, do not act so wickedly. Since this man is my guest, do not do this vile thing. Here are my virgin daughter and his concubine; let me bring them out now. Ravish them and do whatever you want to them; but against this man do not do such a vile thing." But the men would not listen to him. So the man seized his concubine, and put her out to them. They wantonly raped her, and abused her

> all through the night until the morning. And as the dawn began to break, they let her go. As the morning appeared, the woman came and fell down at the door of the man's house where her master was, until it was light.

However, the brutality has not ended. Judges 22:27–30 tells the rest of this horror story.

> In the morning her master got up, opened the doors of the house, and when he went out to go on his way, there was his concubine lying at the door of the house, with her hands on the threshold. "Get up," he said to her, "we are going." But there was no answer. Then he put her on the donkey; and the man set out for his home. When he had entered his house, he took a knife, and grasping his concubine he cut her into twelve pieces, limb by limb, and sent her throughout all the territory of Israel. Then he commanded the men whom he sent, saying, "Thus shall you say to all the Israelites, 'Has such a thing ever happened since the day that the Israelites came up from the land of Egypt until this day? Consider it, take counsel, and speak out.'"

What lessons do the passages from Genesis and Judges teach me? That the well-being of guests takes precedence over all other values? That the righteous man should make any sacrifice in order to prevent the abomination of sodomy? That women are of little value? That both the righteous and the unrighteous are capable of brutality? That God's message in these "parables" is clear: homosexuality is the ultimate abomination in His eyes?

"The Song of the Unfruitful Vineyard" (Isaiah 5:1–30) heightens my sense of confusion about scripture as God's pronouncement on homosexuality, for only the most naïve reader could fail to see that the poem might well be interpreted as a homosexual plaint. This, of course, is not the only reading, but it is a legitimate interpretation. A note in the *HarperCollins Study Bible* says, "This unique poem, sung by the prophet on behalf of his friend, operates on several levels—as a love song, judicial parable, and judgment oracle" (1020). The note goes to explain that in Israelite love poetry, *vineyard* is a common metaphor for, not "friend," but *lover*.

The poet tells us that his beloved created a vineyard on a fertile hill, clearing away the stones and planting the vines and in the midst of it building a (suspiciously phallic) watchtower, but the vineyard yielded only wild grapes, that is, "natural," though unwanted, fruit. The beloved speaks: he has done everything possible to create a proper vineyard. "When I expected it to yield grapes, why did it yield wild grapes?" (5:4) It is hardly a stretch of the hermeneutic imagination to see in this song the turbulent emotions of a homosexual lover whose law is that of Leviticus.

My point is simply that I find it impossible to draw from the Old Testament any moral or theological guidance for judging homosexuality. Does the New Testament help?

In a best-seller, *The Good Book*, Peter J. Gomes's discussion of homosexuality should unsettle even the most adamant fundamentalists or at least make them think. And my point is not that I agree or disagree with Gomes, rather that he should at least mildly shake anyone's beliefs about homosexuality and the Bible. Gomes's first point concerns ritual purity. Leviticus, we recall, is a repository for the laws of ritual purity: clean and unclean foods, unclean animals, purification of women after childbirth, treating scale disease, purification of scale-diseased persons, concerning bodily discharges, slaughtering animals, and so forth. In other words, the prohibition against homosexuality is merely one of many ritual laws. As Gomes says, "[H]omosexuality is an abomination in Leviticus not because it is inherently evil but because the Gentiles do it, and it is therefore ritually impure" (154), as is eating shellfish or pork. Even Saint Paul, the only New Testament author to mention homosexuality, seems to be inveighing only against heterosexual people who performed homosexual acts, not against homosexuality (157).

An abiding assumption in the Western tradition has been that in the text or behind it there is *a* meaning. From the theological point of view, that meaning originates with God, and through digging the meaning out of the text, the faithful can literally read the mind of God. It was Nietzsche who first questioned that belief and who, I must admit, started me on the road to skepticism. Nietzsche and his followers were questioning (deconstructing) one of the most fundamental assumptions of the Judeo-Christian tradition.

Nietzsche has been anathematized, primarily, I suspect, by people who have never read his works, as the philosopher behind Hitler and as the atheistic demon who proclaimed the death of God. Though it is not my project now to redeem Nietzsche from general obloquy, I think he was valiantly honest, and certainly he was tragic and a poet. Be that as it may, he set about to undermine (deconstruct?) what might be called "the Western presupposition": that there is a final Truth to be found not only in profane texts, but also in sacred texts.

A longish quote from the beginning of *Beyond Good and Evil* will set the scene and provide a sample of Nietzschean skepticism.

> The will to truth which will still tempt us to many a venture, that famous truthfulness of which all philosophers have spoken with respect—what questions has this will to truth not laid before us! What strange, wicked, questionable questions! That is a long story even now—and yet it seems as if it had scarcely begun. Is it any wonder that we should finally become suspicious, lose patience, and turn away impatiently? that we should finally learn from this Sphinx to ask questions, too? *Who* is it really that puts questions to us here? *What* in us really wants "truth"?
>
> Indeed we came to a long halt at the question about the cause of this will—until we finally came to a complete stop before a more basic question. We asked about the *value* of this will. Suppose we want truth: *why not rather* untruth? and uncertainty? even ignorance?

> The problem of the value of truth came before us—or was it we who came before the problem? Who of us is Oedipus here? Who the Sphinx? It is a rendezvous, it seems, of questions and question marks. (199)

It is hard to conceive of a more daring confrontation with a cultural presupposition: that somehow the truth is good. One question leads to another: suppose the Truth is attainable? How would we know it if we found it?

The revolution that began with Nietzsche is momentous for theology and for anyone who is interested in scripture because Nietzsche marks the beginning of that modern phenomenon called "deconstruction."

The intermediate step between Nietzsche and deconstruction was the work of the French linguist Ferdinand de Saussure. His first premise was sensible enough and easily grasped: the relationship between the word and what it refers to is completely arbitrary. There is nothing bovine about the word "cow"; it doesn't give milk or low in the pasture at sundown, and any number of other words can have the same significance: Spanish *vaca*, German *Kuh*, French *vache*. However, though the word (as a spelling and a pronunciation) is arbitrary, it is bound within a language system, so that the speaker cannot at random choose any other "word" for the same referent (though, of course, synonyms are possible: e.g., Bossy).

Since language is an arbitrary and a fixed system, where does its value come from? For instance, why do we know the difference between *foot* and *feet*? Simply on the basis of contrast. The German is *Fuss* and *Füsse*. Feet and *Füsse* do not somehow embody a quality of plural-ness, but signify plurality because they contrast with the singular forms.

The meaningful sounds of a language (in the jargon, the *phonemes*) are realized only because of a system of contrasts. The spoken words *dogs* and *togs* are differentiated only because the "d" of *dogs* is uttered with voicing, and the "t" of *togs* is unvoiced. In other words, "d" and "t" *contrast* with one another (and with all other phonemes).

The identity of a word in a language, like the identity of meaningful sounds, depends not on the thing itself, the referent, but on the contrast of the word with all other words in the language. An analogy that I draw from a discussion by Jane Tompkins[14] is illuminating. Language is a game like chess; the pieces and moves have meaning only in relation to one another, within the system called chess, and that system is a set of arbitrary rules. There is no logical reason, except in terms of the system, why the knight should move either one-plus-two squares or two-plus-one squares in any direction; and the knight has no value outside the system. Suppose we want to play chess and find that one knight is missing. We can substitute a paper clip, provided both players agree that the clip counts as the knight.

When we begin to dig the meaning out of a text—the New Testament, the Book of Mormon, the Koran—we are seeking a foundation, some platform of knowledge, a reason beyond which there is no other. Suppose we don't understand the Bible (like all other texts, a structure of differences) or some passage in it. Suppose that some interpretation of a passage in the Bible is disputed. We turn to another text for elucidation; it too is a structure of differences. All of theology is such a structure. And, interestingly, differences are not "something"; they are never present, just as the contrast between the sounds of "d" and "t" is not something, but merely an absence. In other words, "t" is what it is because it is not voiced; voicing creates "d."

In deconstruction theory, everything that we know or can know is based on such absence. The foundation for belief is not demolished, could not be demolished because it was a mere chimera in the first place.

From the complexities of *deconstruction*, two doctrines are supremely important for those who are interested in scriptural interpretation. First, once the writer has inscribed the text, meaning is gone; the reader constructs a meaning from the meaningless structure of differences. Second, no text embodies a final, definitive meaning.

Whether or not the text somehow might convey the intention, the full meaning, of its author, is a question forever moot. The text is simply inert, raw data, black squiggles against a white background, until a reader constructs a meaning from those enigmatic marks, which have significance only in the sense of difference. In the case of Genesis, we cannot assign authorship (unless we assume that God composed the text), and even if we were certain about authorship, we could not somehow peer through the page into the mind of the author.

In a television interview with Larry King, Billy Graham said something like this: the Bible contains answers to all mankind's questions. That, of course, is pretty much the fundamentalist view of scripture and is diametrically opposed to the skepticism of the deconstructionists. In other words, the presupposition that the Book is the word of God and does "contain" *a* meaning is alive and well in the belief systems of millions of Americans. The Disciples of Christ are, perhaps, typical:

> The Disciples share the common Protestant belief that the Bible (except for the Apocryphal Books) is the inspired Word of God, written by different persons at different times under the inspiration of the Holy Spirit. They use the Old Testament for meditation and instruction, a schoolmaster bringing the faithful to Christ.
>
> In common with other Christian bodies, the Disciples have their fundamentalists and their liberals. The literalists, or fundamentalists, accept every word of the Bible as a final and infallible word of God. The liberals believe that a book of faith is not to be taken literally, that it is God's effort to explain his Works to a people learning in the faith.[15] (87–88)

Whether fundamentalists or liberals, Disciples, then, believe that the Bible is the word of God and that it does contain Truth, foundational and beyond-which-not, even though fundamentalists would claim that the Bible is historically and empirically accurate and liberals would hold that Biblical truth is conveyed by metaphor and that, thus, the Bible, though true, is not historical or factual (or that historicity, such as archeological evidence, is irrelevant). Presumably those who read literally and those who interpret metaphorically believe that they will arrive at the same Truth!

In contrast, Unitarians hold that the Bible, like other great literature, presents profound insights and is, in that sense, inspired.

> But it also represents the changing and conflicting ideas of those who wrote, amended, edited, and compiled the Scriptures. Today, some portions are distinctly more valuable than others—and all are subject to interpretation in the light of modern knowledge and personal experience.[16] (266)

In effect, the Unitarians are deconstructionist in their view of the Bible as a text with no eternal, foundational meaning. In the old story, a child asks his grandmother what supports the world. The grandmother replies, "A turtle." "And what supports that turtle?" asks the child. Grandmother answers, "Another turtle." "And what supports that one?" persists the child. The answer: "It's turtles all the way down!"

We are preconditioned to reach certain conclusions about scripture (or any text). Without the knowledge and assumptions that he or she brings to scripture, the believer could not read—in fact, could not communicate with language. On the other hand, our presuppositions to a large extent determine how we will interpret texts. It seems highly unlikely that a conservative member of the Disciples of Christ could ever have a meeting of minds about Scripture with a committed Unitarian Universalist. In other words, scripture is the scene of conflict, misunderstanding, and division.

Dennis Covington tells of a service at the Church of the Lord Jesus Christ in Kingston, Georgia, on New Year's Eve, 1992. Brother Carl Porter was the preacher.

> Carl opened his Bible to a passage in Matthew. *"And as they were eating,"* he read, *"Jesus took bread, and blessed it, and brake it, and gave it to the disciples, and said, Take, eat; this is my body."*
> Carl looked up from the book. "Now, he didn't mean it was really his body."
> *Amen.*
> "They weren't cannibals."
> *Thank God.*
> "Can you imagine me taking a big bite of Brother Junior over there, and him not even cooked? He's forty something years old. He'd be tough as foot leather!"
> *Bless him, sweet Jesus!*[17] (115–16)

One cringes at the thought of the dialogue between Brother Carl and a Catholic priest, the priest holding the doctrine of transubstantiation.

Examples of the difficulties one encounters in reaching agreement about scripture are easy to find, and, in fact, are impossible to avoid. In Los Angeles recently, five believers refused to give their social security numbers when they applied for drivers' licenses at the California Department of Motor Vehicles. They contended that the numbers are "the mark of the Beast," even though in the Book of Revelation, the mark of the Beast is the number 666. These fundamentalists, like a significant group of their fellow believers, hold that the mark of the Beast is an identifying number, without which no one in these last days of the world can buy or sell anything. Rather than lose their immortal souls by giving their numbers, the five went to court and won their case, Judge Diane Wayne ruling that, because of the men's "sincerely held religious convictions that anyone who uses his or her social security number is in danger of not receiving eternal life," the DMV should find another method of identification.[18]

And the news, of course, gets worse and worse when one thinks of the skeptical revolution initiated by Nietzsche. If there is no unitary Truth *behind* or *buried in* Scripture, what is the foundation for belief? More than seventy years ago, Yeats seems to have announced the bad news.

> Turning and turning in the widening gyre
> The falcon cannot hear the falconer;
> Things fall apart; the centre cannot hold;
> Mere anarchy is loosed upon the world,
> The blood-dimmed tide is loosed, and everywhere
> The ceremony of innocence is drowned;
> The best lack all conviction, while the worst
> Are full of passionate intensity.[19]

For me, however, there is good news. I begin with an anecdote. Reverend Jones comes to my house, bringing me The Truth. Since *he* has The Truth, there is no need for discussion; I can simply listen and thus be enlightened. But if I am unwilling merely to listen and want to discuss, the rules of the game change from those creating a monologue to those creating a dialogue, and in a true dialogue, the participants attempt to achieve not only agreement, but consubstantiality; they strive to make their respective opinions into one substance. If Reverend Jones is unwilling to enter into a dialogue, if he is unwilling to strive for consubstantiality with me, our talk and our relationship have ended. And the Dalai Lama:

> Reality may be one, in its deepest essence, but Buddha also stated that all propositions about reality are only contingent. Reality is devoid of any intrinsic identity that can be captured by any one single proposition—that is what Buddha meant by "voidness." Therefore, Buddhism strongly discourages blind faith and fanaticism.

Of course, there are different truths on different levels. Things are true relative to other things; "long" and "short" relate to each other, "high" and "low," and so on. But is there any absolute truth? Something self-sufficient, independently true in itself? I don't think so.

In Buddhism we have the concept of "interpretable truths," teachings that are reasonable and logical for certain people and in certain situations. Buddha himself taught different teachings to different people under different circumstances. For some people, there are beliefs based on a Creator. For others, no Creator. The only "definitive truth" for Buddhism is the absolute negation of any one truth as the Definitive Truth.[20]

I ask my readers now to bear with me and think about a rather long quotation from *A Rhetoric of Motives*, by Kenneth Burke.

> "It is not hard," says Aristotle in his *Rhetoric*, quoting Socrates, "to praise Athenians among Athenians." He has been cataloguing those traits which an audience generally considers the components of virtue. They are justice, courage, self-control, poise or presence (magnificence, *megaloprepeia*), broad-mindedness, liberality, gentleness, prudence, and wisdom. And he has been saying: For purposes of praise or blame, that qualities closely resembling any of these qualities are identical with them. For instance, to arouse dislike for a cautious man, one should present him as cold and designing. Or to make a simpleton lovable, play up his good nature. Or speak of quarrelsomeness as frankness, or of arrogance as poise and dignity, or of foolhardiness as courage, and of squandering as generosity. Also, he says, we should consider the audience before whom we are thus passing judgment: for it's

hard to praise Athenians when you are talking to Lacedaemonians.

Part of the quotation appears in Book I. It is quoted again, entire, in Book III, where he has been discussing the speaker's appeal to friendship or compassion. And he continues: When winding up a speech in praise of someone, we "must make the hearer believe that he shares in the praise, either personally, or through his family or profession, or somehow." When you are with Athenians, it's easy to praise Athenians, but not when you are with Lacedaemonians.

Here is the simplest case of persuasion. *You persuade a man only insofar as you can talk his language by speech, gesture, tonality, order, image, attitude, idea*, identifying *your ways with his*.[21]

Through unpacking this quotation, we can, I believe, rescue ourselves from the dilemma that we have found ourselves in since Nietzsche began to question our ability to know The Truth. In the humanity of Kenneth Burke, I have found hope and a way to live with my skepticism

If the rhetor (i.e., speaker or writer) wants to praise Athenians with an audience of Lacedaemonians, she (the Athenian rhetor) must find a way to *identify* with the Lacedaemonians, *talking their language by speech, gesture, tonality, order, image, attitude, idea*, identifying *her ways with theirs*. That is, she must understand and appreciate her audience (listeners or readers), and in this understanding, the rhetor herself changes, moves toward consubstantiality with the Lacedaemonians.

In a genuine dialogue (which is radically different from an inquisition, in which the inquisitor asks all the questions and the inquisitee gives the answers), both parties must learn and hence change. The logic here is apparent: If Reverend Jones comes to enter into a dialogue with me, it is impossible that he should have The Truth, for if he did, then there would be no need for dialogue; it would be a futile waste of time. On the other hand, if the Reverend and I enter into a dialogue, we move toward consubstantiality through identification, which means that his truth and mine are provisional and will inevitably change as our dialogue progresses. At some point, we may well reach agreement, in which case, we have provisionally established the truth to our own satisfaction.

This apparent foundation, this moment of almost transcendent peace and satisfaction, however, will be taken from us the moment one of us enters into dialogue with another person whose *provisional* sense of truth differs from ours. It's turtles all the way down.

The Truth is, it seems, a grand illusion, creating discord and enmity. Consubstantiality is also an illusion in that no two mortals can ever achieve total agreement. Yet the quest for consubstantiality, through identification, creates brother- and sisterhood, understanding, peace around the human fireside.

8

Conceiving God

> I have heard what the talkers were talking [. . .] the talk of the beginning and the end,
> But I do not talk of the beginning or the end.
>
> *—Walt Whitman*

I'm no theologian, but I have grappled with the logical arguments set forth to prove the existence of God and hence to provide a basis for both faith and belief. Without God, faith as traditional religions understand it would be impossible, but so far as I can determine, logic has not succeeded in proving that there is or must be a God. Belief in a supreme deity (or a first cause or an omnipotent, omniscient being with flowing white hair and a full beard) must come about through other means.

Thomas Aquinas argued that there must be a first cause beyond which naught, a prime mover, unmoved itself or Himself, that originated all motion. This is the so-called cosmological argument. A → B → C . . . X → Y → Z (. . . my great-grandfather → my grandfather → my father → me). In other words, A caused B, and B caused C, etc. Thus, we might say that without A, Z could not exist—but it plainly does exist, and, of course, it would be folly to attempt to trace that existence back through the maze of history to a first cause. (Aquinas did not even have the advantage of knowing about the Big Bang.)

Then there is the teleological argument. In its crudest form, it posits that the world exhibits uniformity and design and hence must be the product of a designer. Years ago my son put the teleological argument to me: "Dad, he said, if just one piece of a mousetrap is missing, there will be no mousetrap." In other words, an intelligence wanted to catch mice and hence designed the trap. But four hundred years ago David Hume demonstrated the fallacy in this argument, and common sense tells us that it doesn't hold water. The Darwinian theory of evolution through chance variation did the teleological argument in, and even if one is a fundamentalist disbeliever in evolution, there is the fact that the chance interaction of a virus with an antibiotic changes the nature of that virus, making it tolerant of the antibiotic. Was *that* event part of the grand design? If one change in hominid genetic structure had not taken place, we can assume that creatures would have evolved, but not the humans that we know. A better analogy than the mousetrap for the evolving and evolved universe is a walk through a city that one has never before visited—say, Vienna. Quite by chance, turning this corner and then that one, we arrive at Demel's and there enjoy Sacher Torte and coffee. If we had failed to turn one of those corners, we would not have discovered Demel's—but we might have chanced on even more wondrous spots.

The ontological argument advanced by St. Anselm in the late eleventh century CE is more subtle. In short, this is it: God is that of which Nothing Greater can be conceived. If, then, Nothing Greater exists in understanding, it can exist in reality, and reality is greater than a mental concept, just as the finished painting is greater than the painter's first conception of the project. But think of the logic here. Nothing Greater exists as a mental concept, but reality is greater than the concept, which means that the reality of Nothing Greater is greater than the concept Nothing Greater. In other words, there is something greater than that of which there is Nothing Greater.[22]

My point is simply this: logic and, indeed, empirical evidence do not and cannot establish the existence of God. Even the genial C. S. Lewis, one of the most popular and readable of theologians, falls short in his logical argument that God intervenes in human affairs.

The God that we know is a cultural phenomenon, having evolved from human longing expressing itself in myth.[23] It was not until 325 CE, at the Council of Nicea, that God became tripartite: Father, Son, and Holy Ghost.

Until the church fathers at Nicea solved the problem, Christians were confronted with a dilemma: How could Christ and God have been identical—both of them God—when Christianity was a monotheistic religion? The Alexandrian priest Arius (250–336 CE) solved the problem by stating that Christ was finite and thus not coequal with the God inherited from the Old Testament. Yet Christians did worship Christ as though he were God.

In 325 CE, the emperor Constantine convened the Council of Nicea to resolve the question of Christ's status and, as a matter of fact, to refute Arius, for Constantine held with the presbyter Athanasius that God and Christ were of one substance. The views of Constantine and Athanasius prevailed, and the Nicean Creed resulted. The so-called Arian heresy, however, has persisted; both the Unitarians and the Jehovah's Witnesses are to a certain extent Arian. The Unitarians worship the unitary God, not the trinitarian, and honor Jesus but do not worship him. The Witnesses do not believe in the Trinity and hold that God and Jesus are two separate beings.

My mother-in-law, Marcella, and my father-in-law, Maitland, had, I think, clear visions of both God and Heaven, derived from Mormon scripture and Mormon folk tradition. I have no doubt that they thought of heaven as a celestial continuation of the farm in Sanpete County, Utah, with their children, their children's spouses, and their grandchildren living either on the farm or in the eternal city of Fairview, each household just a short walk from the old homestead for family gatherings at Easter, Thanksgiving, and Christmas. I wonder if my father-in-law, a modest and practical man, ever thought of his ascension to godhood, as Mormon doctrine promised.

In a funeral sermon delivered just months before his martyrdom, Joseph Smith set forth his vision of God and the great beyond ("The King Follett Sermon"). As a matter of fact, "God was once himself as we are now, and is an exalted man, and sits enthroned in yonder heavens!" If you could see God, you'd find that he, like mortals, has body, parts, and passions. Most originally, Joseph Smith tells the faithful that they can become gods and "ascend the throne of eternal power."

Mormon polytheism seems confusing, to me at least. In the beginning, "The head God called together the Gods and sat in grand council to bring forth the world." Where did the head God and his cohort Gods come from if they at one time were men?

A friend of mine, a church-going Episcopalian, stunned me recently when he said that God had made many mistakes. His belief is, of course, heretical and certainly illogical: if God is omnipotent and omniscient, it is impossible that He could have made a mistake. Yet from my reading of the Old Testament, God emerges as a complete enigma who might well have made mistakes.

In Genesis, we find the dual-natured God who appears again and again in the Old Testament: the majestic and incomprehensible creator of the universe who on frequent occasions seems to have not only the attributes of a human, but also the foibles—for instance, bad memory.

We recall that Jacob married two sisters, Leah and Rachel, but Rachel, his true beloved, was barren; it was Leah who bore him six sons and a daughter, Dinah. (He also begat two sons from Rachel's maid Bilhah and two from Leah's maid Zilpah.) It seems that Jacob tired of Leah after she had borne him four sons, and she had to use the power of mandrake root to lure him once again to her bed to engender the fifth son. After she had borne him a sixth son, she acknowledged God's largesse in providing her with a good dowry so that "'now my husband will honor me, because I have borne him six sons'" (Gen 30:20).

In his preoccupation with Leah, it seems that God had forgotten Rachel, but (with a start, I am tempted to say) He recalls her. "Then

God remembered Rachel, and God heeded her and opened her womb" (Gen 30.22), giving her a son whom she named Joseph.

Again, God seems to have forgotten his covenant with Abraham, for He tells Moses,

> "I have remembered my covenant. Say therefore to the Israelites, 'I am the Lord, and I will free you from the burdens of the Egyptians and deliver you from slavery to them.'" (Exod 6.5–6)

In Genesis 5–8, God does seem to have admitted a cosmic mistake in creating humankind, for

> The Lord saw that the wickedness of humankind was great in the earth, and that every inclination of the thoughts of their hearts was only evil continually. And the Lord was sorry that he had made humankind on the earth, and it grieved him to his heart. So the Lord said, "I will blot out from the earth the human beings I have created—people together with animals and creeping things and birds of the air, for I am sorry that I have made them." But Noah found favor in the sight of the Lord.

Yet even a cursory survey of the Old Testament reveals the repeated assurance that God does not change. For example, Malachi 3:6: "I the Lord do not change." Thus, the dilemma: how can seekers after faith rationalize God's apparent changeableness with his necessary immutability? How can an omniscient, omnipotent deity be sorry for his works? One typical rationalization is that the immutable God can grieve over the wickedness of his creatures. Thus, God does not admit to a mistake in having chosen Saul as king (1 Samuel 15:11), but grieves at the outcome of that choice (*Hard Sayings of the Bible*, 108–9). I think that pretty much leaves us where we began.

I could go on and on and on. Why did God choose that lecherous, murderous David to found a chosen dynasty (2 Samuel 7)? Who were the gods that cohabited with women, and where did these gods come from (Gen 6:1–4)? Why did God harden Pharaoh's heart, thus making the exodus nearly impossible (Exodus 4.21)? Why would God, who from the orthodox viewpoint is the sole creator and ruler of the universe, repeatedly assert his hegemony among other gods (Gen 17.7, 35.2; Exodus 15.11, 18.10)? Was the universe of the Pentateuch polytheistic?

No Biblical puzzle more intrigues me than the Lord's preference for Abel's sacrifice over Cain's. Here is the text, from Genesis 4:2–5.

> Now Abel was a keeper of sheep, and Cain a tiller of the ground. ³In the course of time Cain brought to the Lord an offering of the fruit of the ground, ⁴and Abel for his part brought of the firstlings of his flock, their fat portions. And the Lord had regard for Abel and his offering, ⁵but for Cain and his offering he had no regard. So Cain was very angry, and his countenance fell.

As the reader progresses through the Bible, he or she begins to realize that offerings of burnt flesh please the Lord, even placate Him.

> Thus it shall be done for each ox or ram, or for each of the male lambs or the kids. According to the number that you offer, so you shall do with each and every one. Every native Israelite shall do these things in this way, in presenting an offering by fire, a pleasing odor to the Lord.
>
> —*Numbers* 15:11–13

In a search of the OT under the key word "offerings," I found a total of fifty-six passages that deal with burnt offerings. Other passages, such as Nehemiah 13 and Ezekiel 42, mention offerings of flesh, but not of burning. (By contrast, OT and NT mention fornication only thirty-six times.) More than a little impiously, one might say that the Lord relishes barbecue. More seriously, it becomes obvious that offerings of burnt flesh are the most appropriate and propitious sacrifices and that the Lord seems to favor herdsmen and hunters over farmers. "When the boys grew up, Esau was a skillful hunter, a man of the field, while Jacob was a quiet man, living in tents. Isaac loved Esau, because he was fond of game; but Rebekah loved Jacob" (Genesis 25:27–28 *NRSV*). Only through trickery does Jacob obtain the birthright that traditionally, and by his father's preference, would go to Esau.

The Lord's displeasure over Cain's offering of "the fruit of the ground" and His preference for the fat portions of Abel's firstlings seems to express a racial carnivorousness that, mythified, runs through many cultures. Here is one interesting case from *The New Golden Bough*:

> One night a Huron Indian dreamed that he had been taken and burned alive by his hereditary foes the Iroquois. Next morning a council was held on the affair, and the following measures were adopted to save the man's life. Twelve or thirteen fires were kindled in the large hut where they usually burned their prisoners to death. Every man seized a flaming brand and applied it to the naked body of the dreamer, who shrieked with pain. Thrice he ran round the hut, escaping from one fire only to fall into another. As each man thrust his blazing torch at the sufferer he said, "Courage, my brother, it is thus that we may have pity on you." At last he was allowed to escape. Passing out of the hut he caught up a dog which was held ready for the purpose, and throwing it over his shoulder carried it through the wigwams as a sacred offering to the war-god, praying him to accept the animal instead of himself. Afterwards the dog was killed, roasted, and eaten. [. . .] (30–31)

I can only speculate, then, that the universality of burnt flesh offerings in our cultural genealogy results in the assumption that allows readers unquestioningly to accept the Lord's preference for flesh over fruits of the field. It is this preference that leads to the first murder and to the curse of Cain. As a corollary, one must speculate about the reactions of those from vegetarian cultures to the prevalence of burnt flesh offerings in the Bible. With what presuppositions might a Hindu child arrive at an interpretation of the Hebrew Bible?

My reading is, of course, that of a skeptic. How might a Christian exegete explain God's preference for Abel's sacrifice rather than Cain's? Archer rationalizes thus: God's preference, leading to Cain's slaying of Abel, came about not because of the sacrifice itself, but because of Cain's attitude.

> It would seem that Cain had followed his own judgment in choosing a bloodless sacrifice, disregarding the importance of blood as explained by God to Adam and Eve, and disregarding the principle of substitutionary atonement that later found its complete fulfillment in the crucifixion of Christ. (76)[24]

However, editors and annotators of *The HarperCollins Study Bible* (New Revised Standard Version) say only that "The historical opposition of shepherds and farmers is told here. God favors the shepherd, but the choice comes to grief in any case" (10n). *The Catholic Study Bible* (New American Bible) contains no explanation.

What am I to say? I love the Bible and am a committed reader; but I turn to the Bible as an endless source of poetry, inspiration, and solace, not as a repository of The Truth.

What I'm getting at is my inability to gain through scripture an understanding of God or his heaven. From the Old Testament, the godhead that emerges in the iconography of my imagination is a king richly robed and often surrounded by gems.

> Then Moses and Aaron, Nadab, and Abihu, and seventy of the elders of Israel went up, and they saw the God of Israel. Under his feet was some-

> thing like a pavement of sapphire stone, like the very heaven for its clearness. (Exodus 24:9–10)
>
> I saw the Lord sitting on his throne, with all the host of heaven standing to the right of him and to the left of him. (2 Chronicles 18:18)
>
> And above the dome over [the living creatures'] heads there was something like a throne, in appearance like sapphire; and seated above the likeness of a throne was something that seemed like a human form. (Ezekiel 1:26)
>
> In the year that King Uzziah died, I saw the Lord sitting on a throne, high and lofty; and the hem of his robe filled the temple. (Isaiah 6:1)
>
> The Lord is king, he is robed in majesty;
> the Lord is robed, he is girded with strength,
> He has established the world; it shall never be moved;
> your throne is established from of old;
> you are from everlasting. (Psalm 93)

And I refer readers to Revelation 4, the most astounding vision of God and heaven in the Bible. Since it must be appreciated in its entirety, I will not excerpt a quote.

Not only is the Old Testament God enigmatic, He is also fearsome and a warrior.

In Deuteronomy 7, Moses enunciates God's commandments regarding "seven nations more numerous than you. [. . .] you must utterly destroy them. [. . .] You shall devour all the peoples that the Lord your God is giving over to you, showing them no pity.[. . .] the Lord your God will send the pestilence against them, until even the survivors and the fugitives are destroyed." And Psalm 110, giving assurance of victory for God's priest-king:

> The Lord is at your right hand;
> he will shatter kings on the day of his wrath.
> He will execute judgment among the nations,

filling them with corpses;
he will shatter heads over the wide earth.
He will drink from the stream by the path;
therefore, he will lift up his head. (Psalm 110)

For those who composed the Bible, what could God be other than a regal warrior? The materials from which a conception of deity is constructed are at hand: one's life world. Thus, Joseph Smith, son of a new democracy, conceived of a God very much like himself; as every boy could aspire to be equal and succeed in a free society, so every boy could aspire to be a god.

I paraphrase Nietzsche: "As soon as any theology begins to take itself seriously, it always creates heaven in its own image; it cannot do otherwise." And then the well-known graffito:

"God is dead." —Nietzsche.

"Nietzsche is dead." —God

God clearly is *not* dead, even though believers whom we take seriously and believers whom we consider buffoons ardently profess their faith in *a* God who became moribund in mid-nineteenth century.

How about the rationally conceived "modern" God of philosopher Alfred North Whitehead?

Religion, like science, Whitehead tells us, seeks to find something permanent, to bring order out of chaos, and the Bible is the attempt to rationalize belief, or, to restate the point, the Bible attempts to justify the ways of God to humankind. Read in this way, the Bible is a fascinating account of humans making sense of their universe—and from my point of view, that's a wonderfully satisfactory way of getting into scripture.

However, there are corollaries. First, fundamentalism is always destructive, and, second, founding belief on personal intuition is madness.

The more fundamental a belief, the more God becomes or remains the enemy. Consider Pat Robertson's outrageous pronouncements. The *Los Angeles Times* of June 10, 1998, had this headline: "Orlando on God's Hit List, Robertson Says":

> Religious broadcaster Pat Robertson warned the city of Orlando that it risks hurricanes, earthquakes, terrorist bombs "and possibly a meteor" by allowing gay organizations to put up rainbow flags in support of sexual diversity. "I would warn Orlando that you're right in the way of some serious hurricanes and I don't think I'd be waving those flags in God's face if I were you," a stern-looking Robertson told viewers of "The 700 Club." A spokesman for Orlando's mayor said the gay groups met city policy for displaying flags.

The only adequate comment is "Wow!"

Basing one's belief on direct personal intuition of God is perilous, for the beliefs based on such intuition are contradictory to one another. In other words, personal visions or messages from God lead only to chaos and strife. This "mystic" experience of direct communication with God is quite different from rationally constructing God on the basis of the world that you (and others) know. Of those who claim direct experience with God, Whitehead says,

> For those who proceed in this way, and it is the usual form of modern appeal, there is only one hope—to supersede reason by emotion. Then you can prove anything, except to reasonable people. But reason is the safeguard of the objectivity of religion: it secures for it the general coherence denied to hysteria. (64)

The problem that I have again and again in discussions with committed believers is their unshakable assumption that there is a higher knowledge, transcending reason and history. My "Uncle" Fred, a shirt-tail relative by marriage, had such knowledge. He had a flowing prophetic silver beard and equally prophetic silver hair, and his business card read, "Fred Newbold, Prophet of God."

Prayer having put him in touch with God, he had set out to reform the Mormon Church. While I think he was just a bit off center, or even more than a bit, he had as much warrant for his belief as do other prophets past and present.

Nonetheless, there is knowledge that transcends words. "Mothers can ponder many things in their hearts which their lips cannot express. These many things, which are thus known, constitute the ultimate religious evidence, beyond which there is no appeal" (67). Does Whitehead contradict himself? I think not. As I said in the chapter on prayer, "There are limits to *sayability*." One's deepest feelings are as real as a syllogism or a mathematical formula, but they are expressible, if at all, only indirectly, through the images of art.

The God of Christians, Jews, and Mohammedans is Semitic. The two problems with the Semitic God are precisely his transcendence and the consequent difficulty in offering proof of His existence. Since He is transcendent, our knowledge stops just at that point; we cannot know what is beyond knowing; hence, proofs of God's existence are, in fact, impossible. The logical contradiction: we can know God by viewing the world He created, but since He transcends this world, the evidence provided by the world is insufficient.

The Semitic God may be finally unknowable in any logical, discursive sense, but the God who lives in the mind of the believer is known, for he is the entity that makes the world coherent; he is the value that the believer gives the world. Evil arises when things just don't add up, when discord supersedes "the peace which passeth all understanding."

If God is the organizing principle of the universe, there is an ideal order: the way God would want things to be. It follows that evil arises from discord, that is, from the individual's sense that things are diverging from or contradicting God's ideal order. Since your concord might well be my discord, the concept of ultimate evil or ultimate good is hard to rationalize. Joanne's God does not sanction the taking of human life under any circumstances, but thirty-seven states have the death penalty. John's God demands the execution of murderers, but thirteen states have no death penalty. Thus, Joanne's concord (i.e., good) is John's discord (i.e., evil) and vice versa.

So I'm uneasy with the God of the Old Testament, and Whitehead's God fails me just exactly on the problems of evil, but, thank God, there is the New Testament, in which there is virtually no whiff of the warrior God. The transformation of God is the great Christian miracle, a God who was a fearsome and moody warrior becoming "the Father of mercies and the God of all consolation, who consoles us in all our affliction, so that we may be able to console those who are in any affliction with the consolation with which we ourselves are controlled by God" (2 Corinthians 1:3–5).

This God of consolation, who does not lead armies and who does not anoint kings, consoles me greatly. I know deep within myself and from experience that when all else fails, when hope has ebbed, crying out to the God who is so dimly realized in my own imagination and my own faith is a compulsion, and, as my stories about praying demonstrated, that spectral God does console.

What sort of prayer is that cry of consolation? If it is a genuine petition, there must be a God to hear and possibly respond, for one does not petition a nothingness. One asks a creditor for an extension on a debt or a judge for mercy; one petitions those he or she loves for understanding and forbearance. Of course, it could be argued that this prayer-as-a-last resort is in the same category as a spontaneous cry of discovery, addressed to no one, or the sorts of things one says after hitting his thumb with a hammer. But I think not. I believe that part of being human is the need for the ultimate; in other words, paradoxically, even avowed unbelievers such as I crave the ultimate, long for God.

9

God: The Message

> Hear, O Lord, when I cry aloud, be gracious to me and answer me. "Come," my heart says, "seek his face!" Your face, Lord, do I seek. Do not hide your face from me.
>
> —*Psalm 27*

Since it is impossible that God should convey His truth unmediated from His eternal realm to my finite mind, I can be only a seeker, following clues through the endless complexities of the Biblical text. In the end, I find meaning in two towering figures. From Moses I learn that God is incomprehensible; Christ tells me that God provides hope and consolation. In the Old Testament God, we find humans' perceptions of what they are; in the New Testament God, we find human's perceptions of what they might be.

The OT God is indecisive:

> In a fit of rage, God says to Moses, "I have seen this people, how stiff-necked they are. Now let me alone, so that my wrath may burn hot against them and I may consume them; and of you I will make a great nation." But Moses reasons with God. And the Lord changed his mind about the disaster

that he planned to bring on his people. (Exodus 32:9ff.)

The OT God has a bad memory:

> I have also heard the groaning of the Israelites whom the Egyptians are holding as slaves, and I have remembered my covenant. (Exodus 6:5)

The OT God is vain:

> Then the Lord said to Moses, "Why do you cry out to me? Tell the Israelites to go forward. But you lift up your staff, and stretch out your hand over the sea and divide it, that the Israelites may go into the sea on dry ground. Then I will harden the hearts of the Egyptians so that they will go in after them; and so I will gain glory for myself over Pharaoh and all his army, his chariots and his chariot drivers. And the Egyptians shall know that I am the Lord, when I have gained glory for myself over Pharaoh, his chariots, and his chariot drivers. (Exodus 14:15–18)

The OT God is cruel:

- He orders Joshua to destroy Ai and kill all of its inhabitants;
- (Joshua 8:1–29); commands Saul not to spare any of the Amelikites, "but kill both man and woman, child and infant, ox and sheep, camel and donkey";
- (1 Samuel 15:3); says, "[T]he dogs shall eat the flesh of Jezebel" and her corpse "shall be like dung on the field";
- (2 Kings 9:37); says, "Because the daughters of Zion are haughty and walk with outstretched necks, glancing wantonly with their eyes, mincing along as they go, the Lord will afflict with scabs the heads of the daughters of Zion, and the Lord will lay bare their secret parts";

- (Isaiah 3:16–17); says, "And I will appoint over [the idolaters] four kinds of destroyers [. . .] the sword to kill, the dogs to drag away, and the birds of the air and the wild animals of the earth to devour and destroy";
- (Jeremiah 15:3); orders the Israelites to "Take all the chiefs of the people [who worship Baal], and impale them in the sun before the Lord" (Numbers 25:4).

The OT God is vengeful:

> "The Lord, the Lord, a God merciful and gracious, slow to anger, and abounding in steadfast love and faithfulness, keeping steadfast love for the thousandth generation, forgiving iniquity and transgression of sin, but visiting the iniquity of the parents upon the children and the children's children to the third and the fourth generation." (Exodus 34:6–7)

In short, the God of the Old Testament is very much like many of the unpleasant characters that we have known or heard about—and in many ways, very much like you and me! He is the celestial soul-mate of King Saul.

The God of the New Testament is not a king, but a father, as I used to pray with my Aunt Lucile, "Our Father in Heaven." Insofar as we know Him through Christ, He is perfect in his love. This passage from the Sermon on the Mount is, for me, definitive:

> You have heard that it was said, 'You shall love your neighbor and hate your enemy.' But I say to you, Love your enemies and pray for those who persecute you, so that you may be children of your Father in heaven; for he makes his sun rise on the evil and the good, and sends rain on the righteous and the unrighteous. For if you love those who love you, what reward do you have? Do not even tax collectors do the same? And if you greet only your brothers and sisters, what more are you doing than

others? Do not even the gentiles do the same? Be perfect, therefore, as your heavenly Father is perfect. (Matthew 5:43–48)

Like all searchers after faith and all readers of the Bible, I am confronted with the problem of historicity. If the Bible is taken as history, massive problems confront the reader—for example, Lot's wife being transformed into a pillar of salt (Gen 19:26). Such an event does not conform to what we know (or believe) to be normal human experience; thus, to account for such episodes, we must invoke supernatural agency, and the very term "supernatural" removes the event from the realm of history.

A physician who is a devout Christian or Jew might believe that prayer and the laying on of hands are powerful healing agents, but when speaking as a physician, he or she would not say, for instance, "I prescribed three prayers a day and anointing with holy oil." Speaking as a believer, the physician no doubt would urge patients to pray, but would not confuse the two realms of discourse, medicine and faith. And when one is interpreting the Bible, failure to distinguish history from myth is disastrous. At the present moment, there is no way historically to demonstrate that anyone can be transformed into a pillar of salt or, for that matter, that anyone can be resurrected. Thus, viewing the Bible as myth solves insuperable problems. Those who base their belief on the historical verity of the Bible are building their castles of faith on a foundation of sand.

In the *Phaedrus*, Plato has Socrates explain that concern with the historical veracity of myths is "boorish wisdom." And in my opinion, seeking the historical veracity of the Bible is also boorish. No one asks about the historical veracity of Christ's parables. ("Ah, come on now, Jesus. You don't expect me to believe that the wicked tenants in your parable [Luke 20:9–19] actually existed, do you?"). The whole aim of the parables is to convey truths, not historical data. The whole purpose of the Bible is to convey truth, not historical data. The historical fact that a city named Sodom existed and was destroyed does not lead to the implication that Lot's wife was turned into a pillar of salt any more than the historical fact of the

Trojan War leads to the implication that Athena fashioned Achilles' shield.[25]

In fact, the messages of the Bible are most often conveyed by narratives, that is, by parables. In Numbers, Aaron and Miriam asked, "Has the Lord spoken only through Moses? Has he not spoken through us also?" The Lord explains:

> When there are prophets among you, I the Lord make myself known to them in visions; I speak to them in dreams. Not so with my servant Moses; he is entrusted with all my house. With him I speak face to face—clearly, not in riddles. (12:6–8)

God's speech to Moses conveys laws and straightforward commands and instructions, not the religious principles, attitudes toward life and the hereafter, and foundational beliefs that are the substance of dreams, visions, and parables: Jacob's dream at Bethel (Genesis 28:10–22); Nebuchadnezzar's dream (Daniel 2); the dream of the barley cake (Judges 7:13–14); the parable of the trees (Judges 9:7–21). In fact, the dreams and visions are parabolic.

Jesus explains to the Apostles why he speaks in parables.

> Then the disciples came and asked him, "Why do you speak to them in parables?" He answered, "To you it has been given to know the secrets of the kingdom of heaven, but to them it has not been given. For to those who have, more will be given, and they will have an abundance; but from those who have nothing, even what they have will be taken away. The reason I speak to them in parables is that 'seeing they do not perceive, and hearing they do not listen, nor do they understand.'" (Matthew 13:10–13)

Jesus's explanation may seem puzzling, until one realizes the power of stories. A mere straightforward explanation could never convey Job's "message" about "disinterested righteousness. [. . .] If people will serve God without the thought of the carrot or the stick, then religion will outlast any eventuality" (*HarperCollins Study Bible*, 749). A statement about "disinterested righteousness" could never have sustained victims of the Holocaust, but "The Book of Job" could have and did provide spiritual and moral sustenance.

Stories engage people. The characters, scenes, and events of stories live in the memories of those who hear or read them.

One way of using the Bible is to seek those episodes and passages that bolster one's faith, but though such a strategy may bring comfort to the afflicted and surely will not entangle the believer in the difficulties of the text, that kind of selective reading also drains the Bible of its glories. One reason for the towering eminence of Moses in Exodus, Leviticus, Numbers, and Deuteronomy is that these books engage the reader in the multiple ambiguities, enigmas, and apparent contradictions of the text. The Moses saga is, for me, the perfect example of the difficulties of faith. It is a tragic story, providing the catharsis that humanizes us. The Moses epic dramatizes the imponderable relationship between God and all humans who have even a glimmer of belief.

The figure that emerges from the saga is not De Mille's Biblical lawgiver as portrayed by Charlton Heston, but an often confused mortal who is obsessed with God and is God-driven.

The mysteries of Exodus, Leviticus, Numbers, and Deuteronomy are the essential mysteries of faith and belief—the inscrutability and magnificence of God, the triumphs and frustrations of a half-mad prophet, and the vacillations of those who follow the prophet and thus follow God's behest.

When God chooses Moses as His spokesperson—but "spokesperson" is too bureaucratic a term. . . . When God chooses Moses as his vice-regent on earth, we recall that Moses protests, "O my Lord, I have never been eloquent; neither in the past nor even now that you have spoken to your servant; but I am slow of speech and slow of tongue" (Exodus 4:10). God assures Moses that Aaron has the eloquence to deliver the divine message and that Moses will be the go-between who brings God's word so that Aaron can announce it to the world. As it turns out, of course, Moses never stammers or stutters, but delivers God's word with fulsome eloquence.

There is no Ifa mediating between the seekers after truth and the source of truth, Esu. Moses speaks for God; God speaks through Moses. God, however, shows, in his great cosmic pun, that he is aware of the slipperiness of language. When Moses asks what name he should report to the Israelites when he says to them, "The God of your ancestors has sent me to you," God responds, "I AM WHO I AM," punning on the divine name Yahweh. "Thus you shall say to the Israelites, 'I AM has sent me to you'" (Exodus 3.13–14).

So here is God's first and greatest prophet, the only being ever to speak face-to-face with God, and one would think that the Moses story would clearly justify the ways of God to humankind. Perversely and paradoxically, the four Mosaic books do indeed explain—that mortals can never understand the ways of God, that God is a complete enigma, and that the universe is apparently the scene of God's dice game.

I need not recap the Moses story. One lovely retelling and interpretation is Zora Neale Hurston's *Moses, Man of the Mountain*, in effect an allegory of the blacks' struggle for freedom and equality in the United States. Another is Jonathan Kirsch's scholarly and illuminating *Moses: A Life*, drawing on the Talmud and Midrash to explain the amplification of the Moses myth in Jewish theology. By all odds, the most powerful retelling of the story is, in my opinion, Arnold Schoenberg's opera-oratorio *Moses und Aron*, beginning with the calling of Moses from the burning Bush and ending with Aaron's death. The discordant music and, at times, almost overpowering cacophony of the chorus are unsurpassable as a reaction to and recreation of the Moses story. Schoenberg captures both the mystery and the grandeur of this epic. The first words that Moses speaks in Schoenberg's magnificent work are *"Einziger, ewiger, allgegenwärtiger, unsichtbarer und unvorstellbarer Gott [. . .]!"* [The one, eternal, omnipresent, unseeable and inconceivable God!]. Moses's last words: *"Aber in der Wüste seid ihr unüberwindlich und werdet das Ziel erreichen: vereinigt mit Gott."* [But in the desert you will be invincible and will reach your goal: united with God.] The question posed, then, is "How can one unite with an inconceivable God?"

The four Mosaic books set forth puzzle after puzzle and enigma after enigma, and I believe that that is part of their effectiveness and the whole of their message about faith. Memorable passages in the Bible often have these two characteristics: they are vividly imagistic, and they are enigmatic. They etch themselves on the imagination, and they leave the reader groping for their significance.

One such passage is Exodus 4:24–26. After God has given him his commission, Moses, with his wife Zipporah and son Goshem, sets out to return to Egypt to free the Israelites. But

> On the way, at a place where they spent the night, the Lord met him and tried to kill him. But Zipporah took a flint and cut off her son's foreskin, and touched Moses's feet with it, and said, "Truly you are a bridegroom of blood to me!" So he let him alone. It was then she said, "A bridegroom of blood by circumcision."

In what is perhaps my naiveté, I can only say that this brief episode merely puzzles me. The questions are so obvious. Why did God want to kill Moses? Why did the circumcision and blood change God's mind? What does the episode have to do with my understanding of the relationship between God and Moses and hence between God and me?

If the Bible is God's inerrant message to humankind, there must, of course, be a rational explanation for the episode, and, indeed, commentators through the centuries have constructed a baroque palace of rationalizations. Typical is the footnote in *The Catholic Study Bible* (*New American Bible*): "Apparently God was angry with Moses for having failed to keep the divine command [that all males should be circumcised] given to Abraham in Gn 17,10ff. Moses' life is spared when his wife circumcises their son." *The NIV Study Bible* [*New International Version*] tersely states, "Sensing that divine displeasure had threatened Moses' life, she [Zipporah] quickly performed the circumcision on their young son."[26]

Another unforgettable but enigmatic passage is Exodus 17:8–13, in which Joshua makes his first appearance.

Then Amalek came and fought with Israel at Rephidim. Moses said to Joshua, "Choose some men for us and go out, fight with Amalek. Tomorrow I will stand on the top of the hill with the staff of God in my hand." So Joshua did as Moses told him, and fought with Amalek, while Moses, Aaron, and Hur went up to the top of the hill. Whenever Moses held up his hand, Israel prevailed; and whenever he lowered his hand, Amalek prevailed. But Moses' hands grew weary; so they took a stone and put it under him, and he sat on it. Aaron and Hur held up his hands, one on one side, and the other on the other side; so his hands were steady until the sun set. And Joshua defeated Amalek and his people with the sword.

In *The Bible as It Was*, Kugel records attempts through history to explain "The Symbolic Hands of Moses." Philo of Alexandria (c. 20 BCE—c. 40 CE) explains that the hands symbolically represent the lower regions assigned to one party and the ethereal regions assigned to the other; that is, the position of the hands signified heaven and hell. *Mekhilta deR. Ishmael*, a rabbinic anthology of interpretations of Exodus, says that the uplifted hands bade Israel to look to God and put their trust in Him. *Targum Neophyti*, a translation of portions of the Bible into Aramaic, has it that the upraised hands are symbolic of prayer whereby the Israelites prevail. The Christian interpretation is that the upraised hands are symbolic of Christ (Kugel 365–67).

Whatever the message, the image is unforgettable, in part because of its particularity, Moses tiring and thus sitting on a rock with Aaron and Hur helping him to raise his hands. The battle itself is only background, blurred by the distance of the reader's perspective and the singular focus on Moses.

The "message" that I gain from these passages, dictated by the principle of Ockham's razor, is that God's actions here, as in many other passages in the OT, are simply inexplicable. God is inscrutable. And why should this not be the case? We mortals have only our own sublunar experience and wisdom, which are clearly inadequate for explaining the transcendent.

"The Book of Job" has a Hollywood ending, with the Lord giving Job twice as much as he had before. The Moses saga ends quite differently. The Lord says to Moses,

> "Ascend this mountain of the Abarim, Mount Nebo, which is in the land of Moab, across from Jericho, and view the land of Canaan, which I am giving to the Israelites for a possession; you shall die there on the mountain that you ascend and shall be gathered to your kin, as your brother Aaron died on Mount Hor and was gathered to his kin; because both of you broke faith with me among the Israelites at the waters of Meribath-kadesh in the wilderness of Zin, by failing to maintain my holiness among the Israelites. Although you may view the land from a distance, you shall not enter it— the land that I am giving to the Israelites" (Deut 32:49–52).

The nature of the offense for which God was punishing Moses is a mystery. In the wilderness of Zin, the 600,000 who have fled Egypt thirst and ask for water. "So Moses cried out to the Lord, 'What shall I do with this people? They are almost ready to stone me" (Exodus 17.4).

> The Lord said to Moses, "Go on ahead of the people, and take some of the elders of Israel with you; take in your hand the staff with which you struck the Nile, and go. Strike the rock, and water will come out of it, so that the people may drink." Moses did so in the sight of the elders of Israel. He called the place Massah and Meribah, because the Israelites quarreled and tested the Lord, saying, "Is the Lord among us or not?" (Exodus 17:5–7)

It seems that Moses has followed the Lord's command to the letter, but since his followers have complained (and they are chronic complainers), is it possible that the Lord punished Moses because he failed to inspire the Israelites with absolute faith? Moses's end is as inexplicable as the life and death of other mortals. Thy will be done! We simply can't explain that will.

Or perhaps from "The Song of Moses" (Deut 32), we learn that God is just, and his creatures are degenerate.

> The Rock, his work is perfect,
>   and all his ways are just.
> A faithful God, without deceit,
>   just and upright is he;
> yet his degenerate children have
>   dealt falsely with him,
> a perverse and crooked generation.

This perverse and crooked generation worshipped strange gods and sacrificed to demons, making God jealous and kindling a fire that "burns to the depths of Sheol" and "devours the earth and its increase."

> See now that I, even I, am he;
>   there is no other god besides me.
> I kill and I make alive.
> I wound and I heal;
>   and no one can deliver from
>   my hand.
> For I lift up my hand to heaven,
>   and swear: As I live forever,
> when I whet my flashing sword,
>   and my hand takes hold on
>   judgment;
> I will take vengeance on my
>   adversaries,
>   and will repay those who
>   hate me.
> I will make my arrows drunk with

> blood,
> and my sword shall devour
> flesh—
> with the blood of the slain and
> the captives,
> from the long-haired enemy.

Moses is a titanic figure who struggles against insuperable odds in an incomprehensible universe ruled by an inconceivable and frightening God. We of the quotidian are not titanic figures, but we learn from Moses that we must struggle against insuperable odds in an incomprehensible universe ruled by an inconceivable and frightening God. This is the only God I knew, having met him not in the Bible but in the canon of American literature. The Bible, of course, was not a part of my heritage, nor was it an element in my education, from elementary school through a doctorate. (As I have said, my theological son changed the course of my existence.) I had met God only through such works as Jonathan Edwards's "Sinners in the Hands of Angry God," and Edwards's God was the deity that Moses knew and that pervades the Old Testament. So here is the God of the American literary tradition, the bombastic God who was meaningless to me, merely quaint, one more character among the others (Ahab, Chillingsworth, Hiawatha, Flem Snopes) in the literary tradition and who is still very much alive among such fundamentalists as Pat Robertson and Jerry Falwell.

> There is no want of power in God to cast men into hell at any moment. Men's hands can't be strong when God rises up: the strongest have no power to resist him, nor can any deliver out of his hands.
>
> He is not only able to cast wicked men into hell, but he can most easily do it. Sometimes an earthly prince meets with a great deal of difficulty to subdue a rebel, that has found means to fortify himself, and his made himself strong by the numbers of his followers. But it is not so with God. Tho' hand join in hand, and vast multitudes of God's

enemies combine and associate themselves, they are easily broken in pieces; they are as great heaps of light chaff before the whirlwind; or large quantities of dry stubble before devouring flames. We find it easy to tread on and crush a worm that we see crawling on the earth; so 'tis easy for us to cut or singe a slender thread that any thing hangs by; thus is it easy for God when he pleases to cast his enemies down to Hell. What are we, that we should think to stand before him, at whose rebuke the earth trembles, and before whom the rocks are thrown down.

They deserve to be cast into Hell; so that divine justice never stands in the way, it makes no objection against God's using his power at any moment to destroy them. Yea, on the contrary, justice calls aloud for an infinite punishment of their sins. Divine justice says of the tree that brings forth such grapes of Sodom, *Cut it down, why cumbreth it the ground*, Luke xiii.7. The sword of divine justice is every moment brandished over their heads, and 'tis nothing but the hand of arbitrary mercy, and God's mere will, that holds it back.

Jonathan Edwards's congregation no doubt took his sermons very seriously, but how could an aspiring scholar and great admirer of Mark Twain view them as anything but the ranting of a fanatic? How could a rational secularist believe in the Old Testament God?

In the New Testament, of course, I find God through the image of Jesus, a twofold portraiture, one from the Gospels and one from the Pauline letters. And when I speak of "the Gospels," I include not only those of Matthew, Mark, Luke, and John, but also that of Thomas, which is not canonical. (The Gospel of Thomas was discovered, with other manuscripts, at Nag Hammadi in upper Egypt in 1945.)

With many scholars, I take the Gospels not to be historical, but announcements of the Good News as seen by four believers who drew on tradition but did not personally know Jesus.[27] Whether the historical Jesus was a radical social reformer (as Crossan would have it) or a devout Jew (in Fredricksen's view), the Christ and hence the God who emerge from the Gospels and the Pauline letters give one hope for humankind's future and the wherewithal to exist from day to day in an increasingly impossible world.

From my point of view, the great irony is this: we can know the God of the New Testament only through Jesus, and we can know Jesus only through myth. There *was* a historical Jesus. No doubt about that. Why, then, was it necessary for those who wrote the gospels to turn Jesus into a mythic figure? The short answer is that only through the mythologized Jesus was the conception of God possible to those who had been Hellenized, that is, had been exposed to Greek thought and culture.

I think the Old Testament God had been inherited from an amalgamation of tribal gods: for example, Baal, the fertility God worshipped throughout the Middle East, especially by the Canaanites; Tammuz, another God of fertility; Ptah, the Egyptian creator god; An, Mesopotamian god of heaven responsible for the calendar and the seasons. It was the genius of the Israelite tribes that they conceived of monotheism, an idea that developed gradually, the world of the Old Testament being initially polytheistic.

> . . . on all the gods of Egypt I will execute judgment. I am the Lord. (Exodus 12.12)
>
> Who is like you, O Lord, among the Gods? —Exodus 15.11 "The Song of Moses"
>
> Jethro said [. . .] "Now I know that the Lord is greater than all Gods." (Exodus 18:10–11)
>
> When my angel goes in front of you, and brings you to the Amorites, Hittites, Perizzites, the Canaanites, the Hivites, and the Jebusites, and I blot them out, you shall not bow down to their gods,

or worship them, or follow their, practices, but you shall utterly demolish them and break their pillars in pieces. (Exodus 23:23–24)

I will dwell among the Israelites, and I will be their God. –Exodus 29.45

For what other great nation has a god so near to it as the Lord our God is whenever we call him? (Deuteronomy 4:7)

Do not follow other gods, any of the gods of the peoples who are all around you, because the Lord your God, who is present with you, is a jealous God. (Deuteronomy 5:14–15)

By the time Paul began his ministry and shortly thereafter when the Gospels were composed, there were no whiffs of polytheism; the Jews were firmly monotheistic, as was that most memorable of Jews, Jesus.[28] And God was no longer that moody, vengeful, frightening king; He offered hope and consolation.[29]

I think that Hellenism, the influence of Greek culture on the authors of the Gospels and especially on Paul, explains both the New Testament God and the Jesus of Saint Paul, and though I don't intend to embark on a historical-philosophical-theological disquisition, I do want to explain my own thinking and the result thereof.

The historical studies that I have read pretty much agree that the writers of the Gospels[30] and certainly Paul were speakers of Greek. What about Jesus? He spent his formative years in a society that had been Hellenized, for three centuries before Jesus's time, since the conquests of Alexander the Great, Greek having been well established in Galilee. Herod Antipas had rebuilt Sephoris, within easy walking distance of Nazareth, on the basis of Greek architecture, and as nobility in tsarist Russia spoke French, so the upper classes in the Galilee spoke Greek. Does this mean that Jesus also spoke Greek? There is, of course, no way of answering that question positively, but common sense tells us that speakers of a given language who are in a minority among the speakers of another language do not necessarily become fluent in the dominant language (See Fredriksen 160–64). One of my students, a Hispanic who grew up in the East Los Angeles barrio, spoke flawless English with no trace of a Spanish accent. I asked him about his Spanish. If he went to Mexico, would people assume, on the basis of his speech, that Spanish was not his native language? He assured me that he was perfectly fluent in both languages. And then he chuckled and told me that his parents had been in Los Angeles for decades, but that they had never learned English beyond a few phrases that they needed for routine tasks such as banking or shopping in an Anglo market.

By analogy, there is no reason to assume that Jesus, even though he was surrounded by Greek culture, could speak or understand Greek (except in the limited way that my student's parents spoke and understood English) or even that he absorbed Greek thought or culture.

One important bit of textual evidence for my thesis is the difficulties between Hebrews and Hellenists reported in Acts 6:

> Now during those days, when the disciples were increasing in number, the Hellenists complained against the Hebrews because their widows were being neglected in the daily distribution of food.

In the 80s or 90s CE when Acts was presumably composed, the proto-Christians consisted of two camps: those who did not speak Greek and those who did.

We know Christ only through the testimonies of Hellenized authors, a historical fact that, for me, is momentous. Let me explain. It is hardly news to anyone that the Greek philosophers—Plato, Aristotle, and then Philo of Alexandria—were influential in Hebrew thought; nor is it news that Platonism posited a higher reality of which perceptible manifestations were simply imperfect copies. Thus, for example, the chair in which you sit is an imperfect manifestation of the perfect *ideal* chair. In philosophical terms, the ideal chair is the substance, and the chair in which you sit is an accident.

In the eucharist, the substance is the flesh and blood of Christ, of which the bread and wine are accidents.

In these terms, God is the substance and Christ the accident. How could we know God except through an earthly manifestation? Jesus, though sinless, did not have God's perfection; Jesus ate, drank, and, presumably, defecated, even as you and I; he was mortal, not immortal.

The power of the Christian Bible is that it gives a model for the good life. I believe that the Christian way leads to peace, love, and sanity. (I also believe that the modern American way leads to war, hate, and insanity.) A scriptural passage that I ponder again and again is John 1:17: "The law indeed was given through Moses; grace and truth came through Jesus Christ." God the implacable judge, God the savior.

The Christ of the Gospels was completely loving; he preached nonviolence; and he was a communist, not in the Stalinist or Maoist sense, but in the meaning of the word when it entered the vocabulary in about 1840: "a system in which goods are owned in common and available to all as needed" (MerriamWebster's Dictionary). The American ethos embodies success over love, violence over peace, and individual economic achievement over the welfare of all. The American ethos is profoundly anti-Christian (an idea that I developed in Chapter 5).

The problem, of course, is that the Gospels do not end the quest for our knowledge of God; Saint Paul's musings, theology, and Greek logic follow the Gospels. In Paul's writings, one clearly perceives the workings of a mind permeated with Plato and Aristotle. Paul tragically saw the problem that confronts all true believers: predestination. Logically, it must be the case that an omniscient God knows from the moment of creation until the end of time what the destiny of His creatures must be.

> We know that all things work together for good for those who love God, who are called according to his purpose. For those whom he foreknew he also predestined to be conformed to the image of his

> Son, in order that he might be the firstborn within a large family. And those whom he predestined he also called; and those whom he called he also justified; and those whom he justified he also glorified. (Romans 8:28–30)

Anyone who reads the Gospels carefully finds traces of the Old Testament God (e.g., Matthew 11:20–24), but overwhelmingly He is the Father in Heaven. In the Pauline epistles, one finds a God who must be rationalized. Certainly John was Hellenized, but his Gospel is not permeated with the kind of logical problems that beset Paul. John starts with "In the beginning was the Word," the divine reason that encompasses all and explains all, but John does not then attempt to unravel the skein of God's wisdom. Saint Paul was cursed with logic, and he passed that curse on to us.

In my moments of despair over my life and over the prospect for the future of my grandsons, the Christ of the Gospels beckons, and I want to follow, but have not the strength to take the path down which Christ leads. I have not the fortitude and resolve of Tolstoy's Prince Dmitri Ivanovich Nekhlyudov who, in *Resurrection*, gives up wealth and position to follow his conscience and his faith. *Resurrection* is a great work of art. I am, I think, not being irreligious when I say that the New Testament is a transcendentally great work of art.

This *human being*, this Jesus of Nazareth, sets forth, piece by piece, and acts out in the drama of his life, the doctrine through which I and other mortals can find peace, fulfillment, and hope. But the word *doctrine* is too doctrinal, too sectarian, too legalistic, and for that inappropriate word, I substitute *way*. The journey is the meaning. With Tolstoy, I believe that the "way" is within us, and we have only to follow insofar as we are able. The tragedy is that, for reasons of "practicality" and for reasons of politics and sociability, we are seldom able to wend our way along the "way." We exist in a profoundly anti-Christian society, and we are not—at least I am not—bold enough simply to renounce that society, nor could we escape from it were we to try. We are trapped in—we are part of, complicit in—the very system that denies our deepest longings as Christians. Yet I believe profoundly that Christ's way is the only completely human way. I believe that biologically, through evolution (or, if you will, through creation), we are built, designed, programmed, destined to follow Christ's way.

For a moment, go with me along well-known paths, to the world that Jesus envisioned in the beatitudes and the parables. You know them well, and so do I, but they are worth looking at again, not as words from God but as words from inspired poets to such as you and me. (For poets, just like you and me, know what Nekhlyudov knew, but can say it better.)

The beatitudes are simplicity in itself. Pause for a moment and think about these apothegms.

> Blessed are the poor in spirit, for theirs is the kingdom of heaven.
> Blessed are those who mourn, for they will be comforted.
> Blessed are the meek, for they will inherit the earth.
> Blessed are those who hunger and thirst, for they will be filled.
> Blessed are the merciful, for they will receive mercy.
> Blessed are the pure in heart, for they will see God.
> Blessed are the peacemakers, for they will be called children of God.
> Blessed are those who are persecuted for righteousness' sake, for theirs is the kingdom of heaven.

First, think about the insistence of "blessed are those," again and again. That repetition is powerful. And then think about the audience addressed: the poor in spirit, those who mourn, the meek, those who hunger and thirst, the merciful, the pure in heart, the peacemakers. (Think about this list, and then simply despair for American society.)

The temptation of Jesus is only the most notable enunciation of Christian social doctrine—of the relationship between the polity and the holy life. In Matthew 4, as we recall, Jesus fasts for forty days and is then confronted by Satan, who challenges Him, "If you are the son of God, command these stones to become bread." Jesus answers, quoting Deuteronomy 8:3, "Man does not live by bread alone, but by every word that comes from the mouth of God." Well, says the Christian entrepreneur, "Jesus tells us that bread is necessary. And I spend part of my life making 'bread.' Forgive my little pun. But quoting scripture, Jesus justifies free enterprise." My own paraphrase: "We live not only by things of the flesh, but also by things of the spirit." And of things of the flesh, bread is the most simple and basic and does not represent the American vision of "the good life."

Luke 8:4–14, "The Parable of the Sower." James 51–5:

> Come now, you rich people, weep and wail for the miseries that are coming to you. Your riches have rotted, and your clothes are moth-eaten. Your gold and silver have rusted, and their rust will be evidence against you, and it will eat your flesh like fire. You have laid up treasure for the last days. Listen! The wages of the laborers who mowed your fields, which you kept back by fraud, cry out, and the cries of the harvesters have reached the ears of the Lord of Hosts. You have lived on the earth in luxury and in pleasure; you have fattened your hearts in a day of slaughter. You have condemned and murdered the righteous one, who does not resist you.

1 Timothy 6:6–10:

> Of course, there is great gain in godliness combined with contentment; for we brought nothing into the world, so that we can take nothing out of it; but if we have food and clothing, we will be content with these. But those who want to be rich fall into temptation and are trapped by many senseless and harmful desires that plunge people into ruin and destruction. For the love of money is a root of all kinds of evil, and in their eagerness to be rich some

have wandered away from the faith and pierced themselves with many pains.

In "The Grand Inquisitor" chapter of *The Brothers Karamazov* (246–64), Dostoevsky has this to say about the first temptation. Why did Christ not change the stones into loaves of bread? He had wanted freedom for believers, but "[W]hat sort of freedom is it [. . .] if obedience is bought with loaves of bread?" Mankind will ultimately "understand that freedom and earthly bread in plenty for everyone are inconceivable together, for never, never will they be able to share among themselves."

Satan next challenges Jesus to throw himself from the pinnacle of the temple, for scripture says, "'He will command his angels concerning you,' and 'On their hands they will bear you up, so that you will not dash your foot against a stone.'" Jesus responds, "Do not put the Lord your God to the test" (Deuteronomy 6:16). The Protestant, particularly the Calvinist, ethic in America puts God to the test hour by hour and day by day.

In the final challenge, Satan offers Christ worldly dominion. I will give you the world, says Satan, if you will fall down and honor me. But Christ replies, "Worship the Lord your God, and serve only him" (Deuteronomy 6:13).

If Christ were to walk the earth in this year of our Lord 2004, He would be dwelling among the destitute and homeless on skid row, giving hope and courage to the prisoners on death row in San Quentin, praying with pacifist congregations of all sects, and grieving over those forlorn souls whose life's purpose is getting the next fix. I think that the congregations of most churches would sadden him, their sixty-minute Sunday fix preparing and sanctifying them for the world of getting and spending and obviating the need to be Christian during the other 167 hours of the week. In fact, I feel certain that Christ would shake his head in wonder at the phenomenon of organized religion.

Little wonder that preachers and congregations are schizoid. They have two images of God: the frightening and imponderable God of Moses, who rewards the chosen with kingdoms and riches, and the God of whom Jesus is the embodiment. I choose to believe that the God of Moses was simply the human imaginative realization of what power and glory must be; the God of Moses was the supernal representation of the earthly realm. The God of Jesus was the imaginative realization of a human conception of the substantial ideal, and thus embodied all that was possible for the accidental world we inhabit.

10

Christianity and Capitalism

> Do not store up for yourselves treasures on earth, where moth and rust consume and where thieves break in and steal; but store up for yourselves treasures in heaven, where neither moth nor rust consumes and where thieves do not break in and steal. For where your treasure is, there your heart will be also.
>
> —*Matthew* 6:19

On the afternoon of May 2, 1998, Paul Crouch is in Palm Desert, California, beside a smoldering altar that looks as if it were constructed of cement blocks, with a wheelbarrow as the fire bed. The backdrop for the scene is a huge microwave dish pointed heavenward. Two others are with Crouch: Pastor Ed, a black man in a clerical collar, and a white man in a sport blazer and open collar. The white man has a bumper crop of wavy hair.

"I will bless the Lord at all times. His praise shall continually be in my mouth. Hi, there! Welcome!" says a perky Paul Crouch to the audience viewing this telecast on Trinity Broadcasting Network. A man of perhaps sixty, he is lean and jaunty, with a silver mustache and a head of silver hair. The occasion is a joyous debt burning. "Many of you, thousands of you," he says, "have already planted your seed in the good soil of Trinity Broadcasting, and many of you have written to us and told us you are already out of debt or are coming out of debt."

The ceremony being televised is a debt burning, the promissory notes, mortgages, bills, and liens of the faithful being consigned to the fire in the wheelbarrow that is the center of the cement-block altar. "The Lord just really spoke a sweet word to me today," intones Crouch, "and that is that as this smoke ascends it will be a sweet smelling savor unto Him because it simply says that *thousands* have put His word to the test and are stepping out in faith. This is a faith fire, and faith smoke always pleases God." Pastor Ed interjects, "It gives a headache to the devil, but it blesses the Lord." Crouch: "Especially as that faith smoke goes right up through his [presumably the devil's] kingdom—temporarily, I keep reminding myself temporarily."

Crouch has been appealing for love gifts of $2,000 from the faithful, to help pay for the Trinity Broadcasting center under construction (and now completed) in Costa Mesa, California, assuring those who give the $2,000 in good faith that the Lord will free them of debt within ninety days, an idea that apparently originated with Brother R. W. Schambach, an evangelist associate of Crouch.

As the ceremony proceeds, Crouch ridicules those who put a George Washington in the collection plate; the Lord wants more, wants not a spoonful, but basketsful or pickuptrucksful. Crouch's monologue goes on while his acolytes burn stacks of paper, presumably the debts of the faithful. And Crouch reads scripture.

> [G]ive, and it will be given to you. A good measure, pressed down, shaken together, running over, will be put into your lap; for the measure you give will be the measure you get back. (Luke 6:38)

The $2,000 sums for which Crouch appeals are not, of course, really donations to TBN, but love gifts to the Lord, Who will, in spite of the promise of measure for measure in Luke 6:38, repay them manyfold. After one has accepted Christ's salvation, which is a gift, completely free of charge, the Lord begins to return offerings with interest. Give, and ye shall receive in overabundance.

Pastor Ed offers a prayer, and then, as Crouch and his cohorts burn debts, the scene alternates between the cinder-block altar with the wheelbarrow firebed and Ol' Mike Purkey singing "Fire, Fire, Fire" and dancing around an unidentified site with ancient buildings and ruins.

The action pauses for a commercial about love-gift premiums, a voice-over announcer saying that for $25, the love-giver will receive a "silver" medallion, pictured on the screen, with the TBN crest on one side and a TV satellite disk on the other. For $25 a month or $250 flat, the premium is Holy Land anointing oil, frankincense and myrrh, in a decorative bottle. The real prize, however, is a ceramic Archangel Michael for $50 a month or $500 flat.

Crouch reads off some of the debts that the Lord has liquidated (or will certainly in due time liquidate): $5,000, $40,000, and an unbelievable $400,000! That is certainly "a good measure, pressed down, shaken together, running over"!

Toward the finale, Crouch's "little sweetheart" Jan appears, a woman of indeterminate age who uncannily resembles Tammy Faye Bakker and who has piled hither and thither atop her head and curling around her cherubic face mounds, oceans, clouds, expanses of ash-blond hair, a plenitude which, to her credit, she admits is a wig. She has come to bear her testimony. She planted her $2,000 in the good soil of TBN, and God liquidated a debt of $30,000 that had been troubling her!

This thirty-minute pitch, which had been announced as "Behind the Scenes" at TBN, ends with Ol' Mike Purkey singing "Sweet Sweet Sweet Beulah Land," filmed presumably on location in Israel, Mike alternating with the debt burning in the wheelbarrow.

As Patrice Apodaca says in a *Los Angeles Times* article, "The Crouches preach a 'success' theology in which they contend Christ and the Apostles were actually wealthy merchants. Viewers are told that if they give money, God will reward them with health and wealth" (16).

A question that must puzzle many Americans and that continues to puzzle me: How does one reconcile Crouch's entrepreneurial evangelism with faith in Christianity? Indeed, how can one reconcile the contradictions between Christianity and capitalism?

The March 3, 1993, *Christian Century* published the results of a Princeton University research project on "Religion and Economic Values." In a survey of a representative sample of 2,000 members of the U.S. labor force, Robert Wuthnow and his colleagues found that 89 percent judged our society too materialistic; 74 percent found materialism to be a serious social problem; "and 71 percent said society would be better off if less emphasis were placed on money" (Wuthnow 238). The feeling prevailed that materialism is antithetical to "the deeper human values that have made us a great nation" (Wuthnow 238); nonetheless, Americans cherish their material possessions and dream of having more, a perception that visiting a mainline church only confirms: members of the congregation, one feels, use their Sunday morning as unconscious rationalization for what they do on Sunday afternoon and Monday morning, the visit to church being a kind of counter-balance to real life or a cleansing of the week's grime, the counterpart of washing the family car on Saturday. As Wuthrow puts it: "Critics claim that the churches do a better job of comforting the afflicted than they do of afflicting the comfortable" (240). Though 51 percent of the people surveyed agreed that the Bible provides valuable guidance regarding wealth and its uses, only 31 percent had thought about the connection between money and religious values (Wuthnow 241).

John D. Rockefeller, the archetypical American capitalist, remained throughout his life true to the faith of his father and mother: the Baptist church. Other tycoons of the late eighteenth and early nineteenth centuries built summer cottages at Newport and upgraded their religious affiliations from the populist to the proper: they became Episcopalians. Throughout his life, Rockefeller tithed *religiously*, his contributions to the church in 1882 equaling $65,000 and a decade later rising to $1.5 million. "God gave me my money," he said in 1905.

> I believe the power to make money is a gift from God [. . .] to be developed and used to the best of

our ability for the good of mankind. Having been
endowed with the gift I possess, I believe it is my
duty to make money and still more money and to
use the money I make for the good of my fellow
man according to the dictates of my conscience.
(qtd. in Collier and Horowitz 47)

This God-given ability to make money included both dubious and utterly dishonest practices, such as to make Rockefeller the symbol of all that was wrong with the American capitalist system. By the turn of the century, Rockefeller might well have been the most hated person in America.

Having accumulated his fortune and, apparently, troubled by the almost universal perception of him as the embodiment of evil rapacity, Rockefeller changed the direction of his life: he would use his fortune to rehabilitate the family name and to assure his son, John Davison Rockefeller, Jr., a place of honor among public figures in America. By 1910, Rockefeller's giving was in full swing, his donations totaling $134,271,000 (as compared with Andrew Carnegie's $179,300,000) (Collier and Horowitz 48).

John Junior, of course, provided the inspiration and means for the mighty Rockefeller Foundation, and he and wife Abby were the patrons who brought about the reconstruction and preservation of Colonial Williamsburg.

In 1909, John Junior agreed to chair a grand jury panel investigating prostitution and the white slave trade in New York City. This was just the sort of crusade to engage a Christian, and John Junior said, "I never worked harder in my life. I was on the job morning, noon, and night" (qtd. in Collier and Horowitz 104). His work on the grand jury led him to found the Bureau of Social Hygiene, with an endowment of $5 million and the goal of eliminating prostitution. However, the Rockefeller commitment to morality (and, one must say uncynically, to improving the human condition) did not carry over into business relations with workers.

The response of both John D. Junior and John D. Senior to the infamous Ludlow Massacre is a perfect instance of the morality that allowed American tycoons to separate what might be called their church morality or, if they are not communicants, their conventional morality from the values of business.

The Ludlow story in brief. The Rockefellers held controlling interest in Colorado Fuel and Iron, a mining enterprise and money-machine. The miners, working for $1.68 a day and living in company towns, were paid in scrip that they were required to redeem at company stores, which charged exorbitant prices for the necessities of life. When the men descended into the shafts, their lives and limbs were significantly at risk, for the accident rate was horrendous: for example, in 1914, 25 people had been killed or maimed in Colorado Fuel and Iron operations. In 1913, the miners struck for higher wages, among other demands, and moved out of the company towns to tent cities set up by the United Mine Workers. Governor Ammons of Colorado sent in the militia to maintain order and, actually, to help break the strike, and the company hired goons from the Baldwin-Felts detective agency. Violence had characterized the strike, at one point the Baldwin-Felts men driving an armored car through the tent cities and raking the area with machine-gun fire.

> On the morning of April 20 the labor war that had thus far cost dozens of lives came to its bloody climax. A company of militia that had repeatedly clashed with strikers took up a position on a rise overlooking the tents of Ludlow. The chill wind whipped at laundry drying stiffly on the clothesline and curled the smoke climbing out of stovepipes poked through the tent tops. The strikers stared suspiciously at the men above them. Just after daybreak, a shot rang out from an unknown source, and the jittery militiamen responded by opening fire from their Hotchkiss guns, beginning a battle that would last all day.
>
> As their tents, punctured with bullets, caught fire, the strikers retreated to positions in cellars

dug under the floorboards. By nightfall, the scene was one of complete devastation. There were forty dead and countless wounded. But the worst was to come. For, next morning, as the people of Ludlow emerged from under ground and walked through the smoldering colony counting their losses, they discovered the bodies of two women and eleven children who had suffocated in a cellar when the tent above them had burned. The outrage had found its symbol, and as the news spread, other colonies of striker began an offensive against the mine operators, seizing towns and attacking company outposts within a 250-mile radius of Ludlow. President Woodrow Wilson ordered federal troops into the area to end what threatened to become an all-out war. (Collier and Horowitz 109–10)

John Junior's response to a congressional investigation of the Colorado Fuel and Iron mess was firmly aloof.

The chairman of the committee remarks, "I believe that you are concerned with sociological and uplift movements and that you were recently the foreman of a Grand Jury which reported upon White Slave Traffic. Do you think you might have paid some attention to these bloody strike conditions out in Colorado, where you have one thousand employees in whose welfare you seem not to have taken any deep personal interest?"

John Junior replies: "I have done what I regard as the very best thing in the interest of those employees and the large investment I represent."

In fact, John Junior seems to be standing up for that great American principle, Freedom. "As part owners of the property, our interest in the laboring man in this country is so immense, so deep, so profound, that we stand ready to lose every cent we put in that company rather than see the men we have employed thrown out of work and have imposed on them [by unions] conditions which are not of their seeking and which neither they nor we can see are in our interests."

To which, the chairman of the committee says: "You are willing to let these killings take place rather than to go there and do something to settle conditions?"

John Junior: "There is just one thing that can be done to settle this strike and that is to unionize the camp and our interest in labor is so profound and we believe so sincerely that the interest demands that the camps be open camps, that we expect to stand by the officers [of the company] at any cost."

The chairman: "And you will do that if it costs all your property and kills all your employees?"

"It is a great principle," Junior replies (qtd. in Collier and Horowitz 112–13).

And in the Rockefellers, Senior and Junior, we have it: the dichotomy between Christian (or conventional) morality and the Divine Right to earn millions and billions. As John Lawson, legendary leader of the United Mine Workers, put it in testimony before the Industrial Relations Commission,

> "It is not their money that these lords of commercialized virtue are spending, but the withheld wages of the American working class. [. . .] Health for China, a refuge for birds [. . .] pensions for New York widows, and never a thought of a dollar for the thousands who starved in Colorado." (Qtd. in Collier and Horowitz 121)

Understanding the paradox of Christianity in the American capitalist system must begin with Max Weber's classic *The Protestant Ethic and the Spirit of Capitalism*. Weber contends that the movement in history has been from indulgent Catholicism to tyrannical Puritanism. The Church punished the heretic, but was indulgent to the sinner (36–37).

Calvinism was a dilemma for the faithful. On the one hand, glory or damnation were predestined, but, on the other hand, "it is held to be an absolute duty to consider oneself chosen, and to combat all doubts as temptations of the devil" (Weber 111), for any doubt is evidence of imperfect grace. The best way to build that self-confidence, that faith in one's salvation, is through "intense worldly activity. It and it alone disperses religious doubts and gives the certainty of grace" (Weber 112). "Thus, the Calvinist, as it is sometimes put, creates his own salvation, or, as would be more correct, the conviction of it" (Weber 115).

It follows that a *calling* is an absolute necessity. A man without a calling lacks the systematic, methodical character which is, as we have seen, demanded by worldly asceticism. The Quaker ethic also holds that a man's life in his calling is an exercise in ascetic virtue, a proof of his state of grace through his conscientiousness, which is expressed in the care and method with which he pursues his calling (Weber 161).

The rationale for a calling is, primarily, moral, but if God chooses to reward the faithful toiler with wealth, He must have some reason (Weber 162), and it is not for capitalists to question the ways of the Deity. After all, would not the bestowal of wealth be evidence of grace? And were not God's chosen—e.g., Abraham, David and Job—finally rewarded with things of this earth?

The Lutherans, according to Weber, stove for the *unio mystica* with God, a doctrine that led, among other directions, to Pietism and withdrawal from worldly concerns. This Lutheran mysticism, like other sorts, was paradoxically compatible with empiricism while antithetical to rationalism (Weber 113). That is, one reaches the higher truth through inspiration, not through dialectic or the hair-splitting of the theologians, but the "facts" of the real world are neutral in that they play no part in the system of belief. Thus, one can be a religious mystic and at the same time a secular empiricist.

The Protestant reformers, Luther and Calvin, changed the balance in spiritual life from the rapt contemplation of God or a heavenly city in which spirit-bodies would enjoy a rarefied, carefree eternity, the city being adjacent to a perfect garden in which the elect could stroll. With Luther and Calvin, "The world and its activities assumed a new respectability" (McDannell and Lang 151). These reformers rejected the distinction between the worldly and the religiously ascetic. Activity in the here and now had value equal to that, perhaps exceeding that, of the monk or priest who gave up the sublunary world for the glories of the world to come.

Luther's values were essentially those of a small-town family, but Calvin was an urban creature. "He based his social ethics on a recognition of capital, credit, banking, large-scale commerce, finance, and the other practical necessities of urban business life" (McDannell and Lang 151). Work became almost holy, sanctified.

> Blessed with success, people "receive already some fruit of their integrity" which they read as signs of election for a blessed eternity. Conversely, the poor and those with no luck in their economic efforts appeared damned by God and therefore unworthy of alms. Unperturbed by remorse or generosity, the rich continued to accumulate and invest capital. The incentive to succeed and the devaluation of poverty—once the hallmarks of Christian perfection—fostered worldly optimism. (McDannell and Lang 152)

To account for the phenomenon of Christian capitalism in America, one must also consider the pervasive spirit of individuality, most characteristically set forth by Ralph Waldo Emerson. It is the spirit that animates that great American figure, the entrepreneur. Harold Bloom, one of America's preeminent critics and literary figures says, "The mind of Emerson is the mind of America, for worse and for glory, and the central concern of that mind was the American religion, which most memorably was named 'self-reliance'" ("Emerson, The American Religion" 97). Surely Emerson as much as Darwin prepared the way for American tycoons.

Representative Men is Emerson's version of Carlyle's *On Heroes and Hero Worship and the Heroic in History*. Carlyle lays out the anatomy of heroism: loneliness; dwelling on "the True, Divine and Eternal" (204); the ability to hold one's peace "till the time come for speaking and acting" (242). Greatness is not a specific quality, but a general gift; the specific manifestation of the hero's prowess—as poet, prophet, general—depends on the circumstances of time and place (102–3).

Democratically, Emerson's men are not heroes, but *representative*: Plato the philosopher, Swedenborg the mystic, Montaigne the skeptic, Shakespeare the poet, Napoleon the materialist, and Goethe the writer. As Richardson says in his magnificent biography of Emerson, "*Representative Men* is Emerson's major effort to reconcile the reality of the unequal distribution of talent with a democratic belief in the fundamental equality of all persons" (414).

In the last half of the eighteenth century, an epistemological shift of gigantic proportions was taking place. The search for truth was changing its venue, from the world "out there" to the mind of seeker. This internalization, the solipsizing of knowledge, is a complex story that doesn't need telling here, but that can handily be illustrated. In his "Enquiry Concerning Human Understanding" of 1750, the great Scotch rationalist David Hume said that the mind is in effect boundless, able to conceive anything, "nor is anything beyond the Power of Thought, except what implies an absolute Contradiction" (22).

> But tho' Thought seems to possess this unbounded Liberty, we shall find, upon a nearer Examination, that it is really confin'd within very narrow Limits, and that *all this creative Power of the Mind amounts to no more than compounding, transposing, augmenting, or diminishing of the Materials afforded us by the Senses and Experience.* (22–23; emphasis added)

Compare Hume's rationalistic viewpoint with Ralph Waldo Emerson's Romantic individualism.

The refocusing from the world "out there" to the landscape within the mind and soul of the seeker is nowhere more vivid than in Emerson, who defines philosophy as "the account which the human mind gives to itself of the constitution of the world" ("Plato" 475). The mind talking to itself: the ultimate act of ego, which leads to what is perhaps Emerson's most telling and widely quoted statement (from "Self-Reliance"):

> To believe your own thought, to believe that what is true for you in your private heart is true for all men—that is genius. Speak your latent conviction, and it shall be the universal sense; for the inmost in due time becomes the outmost, and our first thought is rendered back to us by the trumpets of the last judgment. Familiar as the voice of the mind is to each, the highest merit we ascribe to Moses, Plato and Milton is that they set at naught books and traditions, and spoke not what men but what *they* thought. (145)

Everyone who interprets Emerson recognizes this movement inward, this radical individualism. The American critic F. O. Matthiessen says it is "how a single man contains within himself, through his intuition, the whole range of human nature" (7). Harold Bloom speaks of "God in oneself" ("Introduction" 5) and quotes an entry of October 27, 1831 from Emerson's journals: "It is God in you that responds to God without, and indeed is God in oneself" (5).

This radical individualism pretty much defines that American archetype, the entrepreneur. In a *New Yorker* profile, Mark Singer characterizes Donald Trump as "a fellow with universal recognition but with a suspicion that an interior life was an intolerable inconvenience, a creature everywhere and nowhere, uniquely capable of inhabiting it all at once, all alone" (70).

Bruce Barton was author of the great American commercial interpretation of the life of Jesus, *The Man Nobody Knows*. Glance back to 1925, when Barton enunciated the principles of commercial Christianity. The definitive statement is Chapter 6 "His Way in Our World" (100–17).

During the feast at Jerusalem, Joseph and Mary missed the twelve-year-old Jesus. Finding him in the Temple, they asked why He had disappeared. He answered, "How is it that ye sought me? Wist ye not that I must be about my Father's business?" And from that answer, Barton develops a whole Christian rationale for capitalism. In fact, "[W]e understand what those who first heard could not. He was saying that, obedient to God's will, He offered his life to men. To what extent is this principle by which He conducted His life applicable to ours?" (102) Well, of course, we can use the principle to guide our own lives.

> Free men, acting independently of government, pool their skills and money to aid other men in other countries who have been enslaved. The wealth of a family or a corporation is put to work in the service of science, the arts, education.
>
> The principle that he who serves best accomplishes most spreads to every area.

Barton goes on to expiate on the principles of business in the United States. For instance, the CEO of an automobile company, of course, wants to make a profit, but he is also deeply concerned with the comfort and safety of his customers. The great titans of industry—heads of railroads and steamship companies and financial institutions—all subscribe to this "spirit of modern business."

So here is Christ's capitalist philosophy in a nutshell:

1. Whoever will be great must render great service.
2. Whoever will find himself at the top must be willing to lose himself at the bottom.
3. The rewards come to those who travel the second undemanded mile. (109)

Of course, in this Christian-capitalist system, concern with wages and working conditions is downright impious, if not heretical. The scenes of many of Barton's anecdotes are Pullman cars.

James and John, Barton tell us, were real hustlers, called "Sons of Thunder" by the other apostles. When they asked Jesus to give them a promotion, to sit on his right and left sides, Jesus said, "'Whosoever will be great among you, shall be your minister [. . .] and whosoever of you will be the chiefest, shall be servant of all" (103).

> One afternoon in a Pullman car I listened to a wise man who certainly understood what Jesus was saying to James and John.
>
> "I am amazed by some of the young men who ask me to use my influence to get them better positions or increases in salary," he said. "Such an attitude on their part shows an absolute failure to understand fundamentals. I spent many years in one business, with one company. I never once asked what my title or salary was to be. None of the men who made that company ever wasted time over such questions. We had a vision of extending our company's service throughout the world, of making it the finest, most useful institution of its kind." True, the company made this gentleman rich. My own conviction is that he thought of service, not of gain if he served. (104)

I conclude with Paul Zane Pilzer's 1995 interpretation of the ethical and social doctrine so strikingly set forth in the beatitudes:

> God wants us to show compassion and understanding toward the unemployed or the poor not *because* they are poor, but because poor people, with help from those who are already successful, can become rich. And when the poor become rich, all will benefit, because in our modern economy *new unemployment is the first sign of economic growth*. (18)

11

A Pragmatist's Faith

> [T]he work of art has its true being in the fact that it becomes an experience that changes the person who experiences it.
>
> —Hans-Georg Gadamer, *Truth and Method*

I've been through the fashionable French philosophes—Foucault, Bourdieu, Derrida—but I return to and live with our own very American William James and John Dewey (and their successor, Richard Rorty) and with down-home, irrepressible Kenneth Burke, whose pragmatic philosophy of getting along with others is found in Chapter 7.

I think no one has ever discovered a way to base faith on logic or to explain faith through logic. But, then, who would be so foolish as to advance a logical explanation for love or loyalty or hate? On the other hand, one can use reason, as opposed to logic, to explain one's faith and feelings. And this is one of the reasons for my commitment to the pragmatism of John Dewey and William James: they are eminently rational. (So there will be no misunderstanding, I would like to distinguish "reason" from "logic." Logic is a system leading to conclusive proof that may or may not have anything to do with the way the world works. Thus the following is a valid logical argument: *All humans have two heads. Marvin is a human.*

Therefore, Marvin has two heads.) Insofar as my faith is reasonable, I derive it from the pragmatists.

Another reason for their appeal to me is the sheer joy of their philosophy. If you're down in the dumps and believe that the present offers nothing but gloom and doom, if your stomach and mood are sour, if nothing has seemed to go right for you, I can only advise that you immerse yourself in James's *Pragmatism* or *The Will to Believe* or in Dewey's *A Common Faith*, or read around almost at random in the works of Kenneth Burke.[31] (He called them "the Boikwoiks.")

These explanations and applications of pragmatism are ebullient, lucid, wise, and convincing. They are a tonic for the sagging soul. Here is James: "A radical pragmatist [. . .] is a happy-go-lucky anarchistic sort of creature. If he had to live in a tub like Diogenes he wouldn't mind at all if the hoops were loose and the staves let in the sun" (*Pragmatism* 600). James in particular is simply a lot of fun to read.

With John Dewey, I abandon the idea of *a* religion and leave it to sectarian believers and theologians. As for me, "Faith in the continued disclosing of truth through directed cooperative human endeavor is more religious in quality than is a faith in a completed revelation" (*A Common Faith*, 26).

My purpose is not a critique or defense of Dewey and James, but an expression of what pragmatism can mean in the search for faith. Pragmatism offers both a rationale for faith and a basis for hope.

The anecdote of the squirrel is a memorable and apposite explanation of pragmatism (*Pragmatism* 505–6). A squirrel runs up the trunk of a tree, and you want to view the creature, so you begin walking around the tree, but the squirrel scurries around the tree trunk so that you never see him. Have you or have you not gone around the squirrel? The answer depends on what you mean by "going around." If you mean that first you were in front of him and then on his left side and then at his back and then on his right side, you have not gone around the squirrel. However, if you mean that you were first to the south of him and then to the west and then to the north and finally to the east, then, of course, you have gone around the squirrel. The "truth" depends on how you view the situation.

James tells us there is only one truth that even the greatest skeptic leaves standing: "that the present phenomenon of consciousness exists" (*Will* 466–67). In our present consciousness, we can hold a truth that we might well be willing to die for, yet there is no way to prove that what we believe is, in fact, *the* truth. It might seem, then, that our pragmatic skepticism would immobilize us, leaving us in the slough of doubt, inertia replacing resolution. But that would be a misinterpretation, for the pragmatist avoids the unanswerable questions about eternal, absolute Truth and asks about utility. "Is my belief useful? Are other beliefs that I might hold more or less useful?" These are pragmatists' questions about beliefs. James says,

> If theological ideas prove to have a value for concrete life, they will be true, for pragmatism, in the sense of being good for so much. For how much more they are true, will depend entirely on their relations to other truths that also have to be acknowledged. (*Pragmatism* 518–19)

That beyond their immediate usefulness for you and me our truths "will depend entirely on their relations to the other truths that also have to be acknowledged" rescues the pragmatist's idea of truth from mere solipsism; our truths must survive and flourish in the marketplace of truths. A concrete example: an ardent right-to-lifer, holding that human life is the supreme value would be against capital punishment and abortion as a means of birth control. Since this person would argue that the fertilized human ovum, though not a human, is yet human life, the truth held about the sacredness of life must enter the debate over stem-cell research and therapeutic abortion. And since we are all social creatures, we must enter into dialogue with those who hold truths other than ours—those who argue that abortion on demand is a woman's right and those who hold that capital punishment is both moral and pragmatically necessary.

The belief in a benevolent omniscient, omnipotent power governing the universe is not only useful, but even necessary for millions, and there is reason for such a belief (and even, obviously, reason to believe in an anthropomorphic God with flowing beard and silver mane, though I personally find such a belief impossible).

As long as the congregation or the sect holds a belief in God, that belief can be taken as true for that group at that time. It is provisionally true, but it is continually rubbing against other beliefs, creeds, and dogmas; thus it is bound to change, perhaps with glacial slowness, yet inevitably.

James divides the world of philosophies three ways: materialism, rationalism, and meliorism. The materialist is Gradgrindian, wanting the facts, the hard data, the particularities. The rationalist does not deny reality, but wants a grand synthesis, a universal order and reason. The meliorist, however, is a pragmatist, realizing the paradox that everything is true and nothing is true. That is, there is not any idea under the sun that someone has not held or that could not be held to be not only true, but The Truth, the cacophony of religious doctrines being a living example. On the other hand, there is no way under the sun to prove that any of these doctrines is in fact true; their veracity must pass two tests: their usefulness and their ability to survive and thrive in the marketplace of truths (i.e., beliefs).

The pragmatic meliorist does not worry about The Truth (which he or she knows to be unobtainable in any case), but asks about the usefulness of beliefs and grants ideas and doctrines the possibility of provisional truthfulness. The pragmatist lives in a world not of finality and absolutes, but in a universe of hope.

William James, of course, says it best:

> Far be it from me to deny the majesty of this conception [absolutism], or its capacity to yield religious comfort to a most respectable class of minds. But from the human point of view, no one can pretend that it doesn't suffer from the faults of remoteness and abstractness. It is eminently a product of

what I have ventured to call the rationalistic temperament. It disdains empiricism's needs. It substitutes a pallid outline for the real world's richness. It is dapper, it is noble in the bad sense, in the sense in which to be noble is to be inapt for humble service. In this real world of sweat and dirt, it seems to me that when a view of things is "noble," that ought to count as a presumption against its truth, and as a philosophic disqualification. The prince of darkness may be a gentleman, as we are told he is, but whatever the God of earth and heaven is, he can surely be no gentleman. His menial services are needed in the dust of our human trials, even more than his dignity is needed in the empyrean. (*Pragmatism* 518)

A Common Faith, by John Dewey, should be required reading for all religious people. In it, Dewey makes the distinction between religion and the religious experience. While there is no such thing as *a* religion, beliefs and doctrines being so different from sect to sect and from theology to theology, from Catholicism to Mormonism and from Christianity to Hinduism and from obeah to voodoo. But there is a universal religious experience—a feeling of oneness with the world, of peace and joy, of hope—that comes over one in a cathedral or chapel with the choir singing and the organ playing; or in one's solitude, listening to Brahms's double concerto or reading *The Snow Leopard*, by Peter Matthiessen.

It was shortly after midnight in 1996. My son and I, shivering in the damp chill coming off San Francisco Bay, stood arm in arm before San Quentin Prison as we sang with a couple of hundred others "We Shall Overcome." William Bonin, a serial killer, had just been pronounced dead, and those of us who believed in the sacredness of all life and in the futility of the death penalty joined together in this song of hope and reconciliation. This was an intensely religious experience for me. As John Dewey put it in *A Common Faith*, "Faith in the continued disclosing of truth through directed cooperative human endeavor is more religious in quality than is any faith in a completed revelation" (26). Those of us who valued life above death had come together on a solemn occasion, and the mood that bleak night was one of deep reverence. The state ritual of death had brought us together in the struggle for life. That night under the gray stone walls of San Quentin was one of the great religious experiences of my life, particularly since I shared it with my son.

The faith that surpasseth all understanding results from a transcendent experience: a mystical revelation, the awe and love that overwhelms a grandparent on first seeing a newborn grandson or granddaughter, looking out over God's creation from the peak of a mountain one has scaled, feeling the sublime moment of tenderness for a beloved spouse.

Only through art can one express these transcendent moments in such a way that they are at least partially or dimly understood by others.

The Bible is one of the masterpieces of world literature—and much much more. *The Divine Comedy, Hamlet* and *King Lear*, Goethe's *Faust, Pride and Prejudice, The Iliad* and *The Odyssey, Middlemarch, The Aeneid, Moby Dick*—these are great masterpieces, but they rank, I believe, one notch (or several notches) below the Bible *as literature*, for the Bible is not just literature; it is, to borrow an idea from Alfred North Whitehead, the attempt to rationalize the relationship between God and man. The infusion of the holy elevates the Bible to a plane occupied by only a few other texts in the world, for instance *The Koran* and *The Book of Mormon*.

Responding to the sacred is not mere sentimentality, but (I can think of no other word) an esthetic experience.

Soaring as magnificently as the spire of any cathedral is Brahms's "A German Requiem": "Blessed are they that mourn, for they shall be comforted" (Matt 5). "For all flesh is as grass and all the glory of man as the flower of grass. The grass withereth, and the flower therefrom falleth away" (1 Peter 1). "Lord, make me know mine end and the measure of my days" (Psalm 39). "How amiable are thy tabernacles, oh Lord of Hosts" (Psalm 84). "And ye now therefore have sorrow; but I will see you again, and your heart shall rejoice, and your joy no man taketh from you" (John 16). "For here we have no continuing city, but we seek one to come" (Hebrews 13). "Blessed are the dead, which die in the Lord, from henceforth. Yea, saith the Spirit, that they may rest from their labours; and their works do follow them" (Revelation 14).

With its insistently repeated theme, Philip Glass's "Symphony No. 5," a chorale, universalizes the quest for faith:

> There was neither non-existence nor existence then;
> there was neither realm of space nor the sky which is beyond.
> What stirred? Where? In whose protection?
> Was there water, bottomlessly deep?
> —*The Rig Veda*

> In the beginning
> when God made heaven and earth,
> the earth was without form and void,
> with darkness over the face of the abyss,
> and a mighty wind that swept over the surface of the waters.
> —*Genesis*

> My limbs fail and my mouth is parched.
> My body is shaken and my hair stands on end.
> The bow Gandiva slips from my hand
> [and my skin is on fire.]
> I cannot hold myself steady;
> my mind seems to whirl.
> —*The Bhagavad Gita*

T. S. Eliot's "Choruses from the Rock" is one of the great heart-broken cries from a person of faith who lives in a faithless age. In one chorus, a male voice sings,

> A Cry from the North, from the West and from the South
> Where thousands travel daily to the timekept city;
> Where My Word is unspoken,

> In the land of lobelias and tennis flannels
> The rabbit shall burrow and the thorn revisit,
> The nettle shall flourish on the gravel court,
> And the wind shall say: "Here were decent godless people:
> Their only monument the asphalt road
> And a thousand lost golf balls."

All of these magnificent works, and many others, are illuminated by the glow from holy texts that embody humans' questions about the beginning and the end and that serve as the rocks upon which edifices of faith are built.

There is a state of mind that might be called "religious awe," which comes about, in my case, as a result of immersion in art.

Art? I mean not only Shakespeare, but also the folk tales and traditional stories that are passed from generation to generation. I mean not only Beethoven, but also the songs our two-year-old grandson sings to us ("Oh, where, oh, where has the little dog gone?") and the great hymns that are so important a part of the Christian tradition. I mean not only Chartres or the Salisbury Cathedral, but also the home my wife has designed and decorated. I mean not only Rembrandt, but also the finger-painting that my now nineteen-year-old grandson did when he was a tot in day care.

An anecdote helps explain my theory of art.

My wife and I were viewing an exhibit of American minimalist art in the National Gallery in London. We were standing before and puzzling over a huge canvas that was simply pristine white with the exception of one black dot in the center. A young woman standing next to us shook her head and asked me, "Is that art?" I replied, "Of course it is. It's hanging the National Gallery, isn't it?"

Art is a work or experience (dream, meditation) that you "frame" and contemplate for reasons other than "logic," immediate utility, information, and so on. The Metro Goldwyn Mayer slogan was, and perhaps still is, *Ars gratia artis*: art for art's sake. But for you and for me, art does have a real utility, which might be expressed in this way: Art for the sake of faith. Art for the sake of hope.

Come with me for a visit to two great American writers who express all I have of faith and hope: Wallace Stevens[32] and Walt Whitman.[33]

I begin with one of my favorite of Stevens's poems: his "portrait" of St. Ursula, the fourth century Christian who in legend was martyred along with 11,000 virgins who followed her on a pilgrimage to the Holy Land. Ursula prepares an offering of radishes and roses to God, but God is so busy with his own garden that he hardly notices Ursula's gift.

> Ursula, in a garden, found
> A bed of radishes.
> She kneeled upon the ground
> And gathered them,
> With flowers around,
> Blue, gold, pink, and green.
>
> She dressed in red and gold brocade
> And in the grass an offering made
> Of radishes and flowers.
>
> She said, "My dear,
> Upon your altars,
> I have placed
> The marguerite and coquelicot,
> And roses
> Frail as April snow.
> But here," she said,
> "Where none can see,
> I make an offering, in the grass,
> Of radishes and flowers."
> And then she wept
> For fear the Lord would not accept.
>
> The good Lord in His garden sought
> New leaf and shadowy tinct,

> And they were all His thought.
> He heard her low accord,
> Half prayer and half ditty,
> And He felt a subtle quiver,
> That was not heavenly love,
> Or pity.
>
> This is not writ
> In any book.[34]

The Lord is neither cruel nor malevolent, simply indifferent to the hopes and dreams of his creatures. At last, in her devotion and piety, Ursula made the supreme sacrifice, she and her 11,000 virgins having been martyred in Cologne by the Huns. Did the Lord bring this end about? Or did He merely feel a subtle quiver that was neither love nor pity? The glory of the poem, of course, is not its "message," but the unforgettable images through which that "message" is conveyed. Saint Ursula offering up radishes and roses while God tends His own garden. Saint Ursula's devotion to this enigmatic God.

In Stevens's "The Woman That Had More Babies Than That," we find God the Acrobat observing the Universal Machine and perceiving "The need for a thesis, a music constant to move" (202). But there is also a mother desiring a fiery lullaby at the end, whose voice is still in the ears of those with bald heads. While the Acrobat dispassionately views the never-ending cycle of the surf breaking and receding, there is always a mother to give one both hope and faith. As Robert Frost said, "The earth's the right place for love."

God the indifferent gardener, God the acrobat—and God the emperor of ice cream. In what is probably his best-known poem, "The Emperor of Ice Cream," Stevens portrays a wake, at which a roller of big cigars whips concupiscent curds while others cover the face of the deceased with a sheet taken from a deal dresser with three missing knobs, a sheet on which she, whose horny feet protrude, once embroidered a fantail. On this corpse, "Let the lamp affix its beam. / The only emperor is the emperor of ice-cream" (50). Ice-cream is sweet and soothing, but it rapidly melts, and it is not a substantial food. The Emperor of Ice-Cream, Stevens seems to be telling us, is sweet, soothing, and insubstantial; he dispassionately observes the mortal world, symbolized by the wake for her of the horny feet.

> Call the roller of big cigars,
> The muscular one, and bid him whip
> In kitchen cups concupiscent curds.
> Let the wenches dawdle in such dress
> As they are used to wear, and let the boys
> Bring flowers in last month's newspapers.
> Let be be finale of seem.
> The only emperor is the emperor of ice-cream.
>
> Take from the dresser of deal,
> Lacking the three glass knobs, that sheet
> On which she embroidered fantails once
> And spread it so as to cover her face.
> If her horny feet protrude, they come
> To show how cold she is, and dumb.
> Let the lamp affix its beam.
> The only emperor is the emperor of ice-cream.

Of the poem, Stevens says, "I think I should select from my poems as my favorite *The Emperor of Ice Cream*. This wears a deliberately commonplace costume, and yet seems to me to contain something of the essential gaudiness of poetry. [. . .]" The setting is commonplace: a somewhat shabby dwelling, perhaps an apartment. The conception is gaudy, with its cigar-roller MC, its emperor God, and its corpse with horny feet. In fact, one might say that Stevens repeatedly expresses the commonplaces of life's problems in the gaudiness of poetry.

His antic view of God is a witty and memorable way to express his skepticism, but taken as whole, his collected poems set forth a mellow and slightly melancholy hopefulness, in that all hope must be in the context of mortality. He says, "Death is the mother of beauty, mystical, / Within whose burning bosom we devise / Our earthly mothers waiting, sleeplessly" (55). Beauty provides the stuff we need to experience a life that must end; through beauty, we learn to face death.

On a Sunday morning, a woman sitting in the warmth of the sun, the aroma of coffee and oranges permeating the air and the "green freedom" of a cockatoo adding a typically Stevensian flash of color, feels "the dark / Encroachment of that old catastrophe" (53).

> She says, "I am content when wakened birds,
> Before they fly, test the reality
> Of misty fields, by their sweet questionings;
> But when the birds are gone, and their warm fields
> Return no more, where, then, is paradise?"
> There is not any haunt of prophesy,
> Nor any old chimera of the grave,
> Neither the golden underground, nor isle
> Melodious, where spirits gat them home,
> Nor visionary south, nor cloudy palm
> Remote on heaven's hill, that has endured
> As April's green endures; or will endure
> Like her remembrance of awakened birds,
> Or her desire for June and evening, tipped
> By the consummation of the swallow's wings.

As for this universe that we inhabit and that swirls about us—we make it! The singer is the "single artificer" of the world in which he or she sings, and the only reality is the song itself. As William James said, we are certain only of this: "that the present phenomenon of consciousness exists." Philosophers, with their dark cuffs on voluminous cloaks, ought to think hard before they declare the "Eureka!" of Truth discovered. It could well be "that their mistress / Is no gaunt fugitive phantom. / She might, after all, be a wanton, / Abundantly beautiful, eager, / Fecund" (20–21). The real Truth might be as palpable as one's mistress, not a misty chimera. The Truth is lived in this world through which men and women pass, only "the dew upon their feet" manifesting whither they go (56).

As for sects, well, the bells in all the churches sound the same. "Each sexton has his sect. The bells have none" (394). "Each truth is a sect though no bells ring for it. / And the bells belong to the sextons, after all, / As they jangle and dangle and kick their feet" (394).

Walt Whitman as poet is radically different from Wallace Stevens; where Stevens is always imagistic and allusive, Whitman is often direct and even oratorical.

Whitman expresses an exuberant love of life and of humankind and, assuming the persona of a learned professor lecturing to his students, makes this glowing love

The Base of All Metaphysics

And now gentlemen,
A word I give to remain in your memories and minds,
As base and finalè too for all metaphysics.

(So to the students the old professor,
At the close of his crowded course.)

Having studied the new and antique, the Greek and Germanic systems,
Kant having studied and stated, Fichte and Schelling and Hegel,
Stated the lore of Plato, and Socrates greater than Plato,
And greater than Socrates sought and stated, Christ divine having studied long,
I see reminiscent to-day those Greek and German systems,
See the philosophies all, Christian churches and tenets see,
Yet underneath Socrates clearly see, and underneath Christ the divine I see,
The dear love of man for his comrade, the attraction of friend to friend,
Of the well-married husband and wife, of children and parents,
Of city for city and land for land.

There is a joy in living—the French call it *joie de vivre*—that makes heaven unnecessary, the here-and-now being so replete with love and hope that the hereafter is below the level of one's consciousness. Whitman sings of the body electric: "That of the male is perfect, and that of the female is perfect" (251). Whitman avows his belief in the appetites: "Seeing hearing and feeling are miracles, and each part and tag of me is a miracle" (51). Whitman celebrates and revels in the world around him:

> Walking the path worn in the grass and beat
>   through the leaves of the brush,
> Where the quail is whistling betwixt the woods
>   and the wheat-lot,
> Where the bat flies in the Seventh-month eve, where
>   the great goldbug drops through the dark,
> Where the brook puts out of the roots of the old
>   tree and flows to the meadow,
> Where cattle stand and shake away flies with
>   the tremulous shuddering of their hides. [. . .]
>   (220)

As for God and Heaven. "I hear and behold God in every object, yet I understand God not in the least [. . .] " (85). In the dry language of exposition: God is manifest in His creation and creatures, but since He transcends them, they are not pages in a book setting forth the nature of God; the universe is a cryptic, Gnostic message as enigmatic and as intriguing and inspiring as "The Gospel of Thomas."

Whitman senses eternity—lives in the everlasting!—without pearly gates or Elysian fields, without choirs of angels or the judgment seat. The eternal now is enough for him,

> Content with the present, content with the past,
> By my side or back of me Eve following,
> Or in front, and I following her just the same.
>   (248)

As he crosses Brooklyn ferry, he muses:

> It avails not, time nor place—distance avails not,
> I am with you, you men and women of a genera-
> tion, or ever so many generations hence,
> Just as you feel when you look on the river and sky,
> so I felt,
> Just as any of you is one of the living crowd, I was
> one of a crowd,
> Just as you are refreshed by the gladness of the river
> and the bright flow, I was refreshed,
> Just as you stand and lean on the rail, yet hurry
> with the swift current, I stood yet was hurried,
> Just as you look on the numberless masts of ships
> and the thick-stemm'd pipes of steamboats, I
> looked. (308–9)

Whitman has only what the most devout Christian, Jew, Muslim, or Hindu has: hope. Plus honesty with himself. He knows that God and the gods have been fabricated by "the old cautious hucksters" (73), and he takes them "for what they are worth, and not a cent more" (74), "[a]dmitting they were alive and did the work of their day" (74); however, "The most they offer for mankind and eternity [is] less than the spirit of my own seminal wet" (73).

In his great essay "Democratic Vistas," Whitman expresses his hope for the future of this nation that he so loved, "Nor is that hope unwarranted" (929) Without hope for the future of this nation, I have no idea how I could endure the present. Statistics are a funeral dirge: forty million Americans without health insurance; the skies becoming murkier and murkier with effluent from hulking autos and reeking industries; the devastation of the earth for the sake of profit *for the few*. . . . I am living the last bittersweet months or years of my own life with a woman who grows more dear to me minute by minute. The hours of this autumnal here-and-now grow more precious with each dawn and each dusk, and hope for my grandchildren, for the future, glimmers in the dark hours as I lie wakeful next to my gently breathing wife.

Even in these dark years of a ravaged earth, of international capitalism enslaving third-world masses, of a California death row with more than 600 souls festering in the slow mills of a justice system gone awry, of a presidency achieved through baseness viewed complacently by the masses, of a president who declares perpetual war on the world, of an economic system in which five percent of the population has sixty percent of the wealth, of an age in which scientists can patent the "humouse" (human + mouse), even in such an age I have hope—and that is all I have, but that must be enough.

Notes

¹ The Book of Mormon is Joseph Smith's translation of the golden plates that he found in the Hill Cumorah; Doctrine and Covenants is revelations to Joseph Smith and two other Church presidents from God; Pearl of Great Price is a collection of doctrinal statements, writings, and translations, including the notorious Book of Abraham, which Joseph Smith "translated" from Egyptian papyri, but which has proved to be a hoax.

² Lehman did plan to hold dances in the coolness of the cave.

³ "Cy Est Pourtraicte, Madame Ste Ursule, et Les Unze Mille Vierges."

⁴ Scholastica was the sister of Benedict of Nursia, founder of the Benedictine order in mid-sixth century.

⁵ In response, one can only say, "Wow!"

⁶ 1Cor 13:12.

⁷ 1Cor.13:12.

⁸ In a marginal note on my manuscript, Dr. Steven Byars said, "Arguably, Augustine is inspired in his anagogy by the Paul, who held *all* Scripture to be well suited for this purpose."

⁹ "When [Ambrose] read, his eyes scanned the page and his heart explored the meaning, but his voice was silent and his tongue was still" (*Confessions* VI.3). Thus, Ambrose is the perfect symbol for the transition from the oral to the literate culture, from the ages of giving voice to text to the advent of silent reading.

¹⁰ Frag = sentence fragment; CF = comma fault; Par = faulty parallelism; Sp = spelling.

¹¹ Kenneth Burke would have spoken of Augustine's *alembification* of the Neoplatonic doctrine.

¹² Henry Louise Gates. *The Signifying Monkey*. New York: Oxford UP, 1988. 3-43.

¹³ See, for instance, David K. Rensberger, "John: Introduction," *The HarperCollins Study Bible*. (New York: HarperCollins, 1993), 2012.

¹⁴ Jane Tompkins. "A Short Course in Post-Structuralism." *College English* 50 (1989): 733-47.

¹⁵ James E. Craig and Robert L. Friedly. "Who Are the Disciples of Christ (*Christian Church*)?" Leo Rosten, ed. *The Religions of America*. New York: Simon & Schuster, 1975. 83-95.

¹⁶ Karl M. Chworowsky and Christopher Gist Raible. "What Is a Unitarian Universalist?" Leo Rosten, ed. *The Religions of America*. New York: Simon & Schuster, 1975. 263-76.

¹⁷ Dennis Covington. *Salvation on Sand Mountain*. New York: Penguin, 1994.

¹⁸ John Dart. "Religious Objections to DMV Upheld in LA." *Los Angeles Times*. Oct. 25, 1997. A12.

¹⁹ W. B. Yeats. "The Second Coming." *The Collected Poems of W. B. Yeats*. New York: Macmillan, 1959. 184-85.

²⁰ Dalai Lama. "The Dalai Lama on China, Hatred, and Optimism: A Conversation with Robert Thurman." *Mother Jones* (Nov.-Dec. 1997): 28-31; 82-83. 83.

²¹ Kenneth Burke. *A Rhetoric of Motives*. 1950. Berkeley: U of California P, 1969. 55. Emphasis added.

²² In my summary of logical arguments I have relied on Louis P. Pojman's *Philosophy of Religion*, pp. 1-93.

23 If you want to know about God—how God has been perceived through history and how philosophers have rationalized the concept of God—I refer you to *A History of God*, by Karen Armstrong, and *God: A Biography*, by Jack Miles. If you want to follow Western humankind's perception of heaven, I refer you to *Heaven: A History*, by Colleen McDannell and Bernhard Lang. Excellent books. Scholarly, but not stodgy, not thorny with footnotes.

²⁴ In his exegesis, Archer apparently follows Augustine in *The City of God*: "[John] thus gives us to understand that God did not respect [Cain's] offering because it was not rightly 'distinguished'

in this, that he gave to God something of his own but kept himself to himself. For this all do who follow not God's will but their own, who live not with an upright but a crooked heart, and yet offer to God such gifts as they suppose will procure from Him that He aid them not by healing but by gratifying their evil passions" (485).

[25] *The Historian and the Believer*, by Van A. Harvey, should be required reading for anyone interested in the intellectual and ethical problems of history in relation to the Bible. *The Bible Unearthed*, by Israel Finkelstein and Neil Asher Silberman, reviews the archaeological evidence for the Bible's historicity, proving conclusively, in my opinion, that the Old Testament is not a historical document. In *Excavating Jesus*, John Dominic Crossan and Jonathan L. Reed set forth the archaeological evidence that makes the historicity of the New Testament much more than a little doubtful.

[26] For a more elaborate explanation, see Kugel, *The Bible as It Was*, 305-8.

[27] Marcus J. Borg, *Jesus: A New Vision* and *Jesus in Contemporary Scholarship*; John Dominic Crossan, *Jesus: A Revolutionary Biography*; Paula Fredriksen, *Jesus of Nazareth, King of the Jews*; A. N. Wilson, *Jesus: A Life*.

[28] As Chapter 6 points out, the monotheistic Jews started to worship Christ as though he were God, and this led to the controversy that the Council of Nicea attempted to resolve.

[29] In *Christ* (2001), Jack Miles advances an intriguing and, in my view plausible, thesis regarding the transformation of God in the New Testament. God the *miles gloriosus*, the warrior king and conqueror, had been defeated one last time: the Romans had taken the Holy Land. God, then, had to accommodate, and He did so by becoming the God of forgiveness and meekness. He will no longer defeat his enemies, but will turn the other cheek, achieving victory in the hereafter, but not on earth. God becomes Jesus.

[30] With the majority of contemporary Biblical scholars, I assume that the Gospels were not written by disciples of Christ and were composed decades after the crucifixion. For convenience, I will use the traditional authorial names, Matthew, Mark, Luke, and John.

[31] Among modern philosophers, Burke is usually not considered a pragmatist. (In fact, some would not consider him a philosopher at all.) However, when one distills from the copiousness of his works a summary of uses, he does seem to be a pragmatist.

[32] For all quotations from and references to the works, see *Wallace Stevens: Collected Poetry and Prose*, The Library of America.

[33] For all quotations from and references to the works, see *Whitman: Complete Poetry and Collected Prose*, The Library of America.

[34] It occurs to me that my offering, under Aunt Lucile's guidance, was very much like that of St. Ursula. Remember the paragraph from my first chapter: Aunt Lucile was dear to me, taking me, when I was a preschooler, to Liberty Park for endless rides on the merry-go-round, helping me plant onions and radishes in her backyard, taking me to the S. H. Kress five-and-dime lunch counter for egg salad sandwiches—and we bowed our heads and prayed before we ate.

Bibliography

Alter, Robert. *The Art of Biblical Narrative.* New York: Basic Books, 1983.
Archer, Gleason L. *Encyclopedia of Bible Difficulties.* Grand Rapids, MI: Regency, 1982.
Arendt, Hannah. *Eichmann in Jerusalem: A Report on the Banality of Evil.* New York: Penguin, 1994.
Armstrong, Karen. *A History of God.* New York: Ballantine, 1993.
—. *In the Beginning.* New York: Knopf, 1996.
Augustine, Saint. *The City of God.* Trans. Marcus Dodds. Intro. Thomas Merton. New York: Modern Library, 1993.
—. *Confessions.* Trans. R. S. Pine-Coffin. London: Penguin, 1961.
—. *On Christian Doctrine.* Trans. D. W. Robertson, Jr. New York: Liberal Arts Press, 1958.
Barton, Bruce. *The Man Nobody Knows.* 1925. Indianapolis: Charter, 1962.
Bloom, Harold. "Emerson: The American Religion." Bloom, 97–121.
—. "Introduction." Bloom, 1–11.
—. ed. *Ralph Waldo Emerson.* New York: Chelsea, 1985.
Book of Mormon. In *Book of Mormon, Doctrine and Covenants, Pearl of Great Price.* Salt Lake City: The Church of Jesus Christ of Latter-day Saints, 1981. 1–535
Borg, Marcus J. *Jesus: A New Vision.* New York: HarperSanFrancisco, 1991.
—. *Jesus in Contemporary Scholarship.* Valley Forge, PA: Trinity, 1994.

Breitman, Richard. *The Architect of Genocide: Himmler and the Final Solution.* London: Bodley Head, 1991.

Burke, Kenneth. *A Rhetoric of Motives.* 1950. Berkeley: U of California P, 1969.

Chworowsky, Karl M., and Christoper Gist Raible. "What Is a Unitarian Universalist?" Rosten. 263–76.

Colson, Charles. *Who Speaks for God?* Westchester, IL: Crossway, 1985.

Cook, E. U. *The First Mortgage.* Chicago: Rhodes & McClure, 1896.

Covington, Dennis. *Salvation on Sand Mountain.* New York: Penguin, 1994.

Craig, James E., and Robert L. Friedly. "Who Are the Disciples of Christ (Christian Church)?" Rosten, 83–95.

Crossan, John Dominic. *Jesus: A Revolutionary Biography.* New York: HarperCollins, 1995.

Crossan, John Dominic, and Jonathan L. Reed. *Excavating Jesus.* New York: HarperSanFrancisco, 2001.

Dalai Lama. "The Dalai Lama on China, Hatred, the Optimism: A Conversation with Robert Thurman." *Mother Jones* (Nov.-Dec. 1997): 28–31; 82–83.

Dart, John. "Religious Objections to DMV Upheld in LA." *Los Angeles Times.* Oct. 25, 1997. A12.

Dewey, John. *A Common Faith.* New Haven: Yale UP, 1991.

Dostoevsky, Fyodor. *The Brothers Karamazov.* Trans. Richard Pevear and Larissa Volokhonsky. New York: Vintage, 1991.

—. *Resurrection.* Trans. Rosemary Edmonds. New York: Penguin, 1966.

Emerson, Ralph Waldo. "Plato; or, The Philosopher." *The Writings of Ralph Waldo Emerson.* 471–98.

—. "Self-Reliance." *The Writings of Ralph Waldo Emerson.* 145–69.

Emerson, Ralph Waldo. *The Writings of Ralph Waldo Emerson.* Ed. Brooks Atkinson. New York: Modern Library, 1950.

Fest, Joachim. *Speer: The Final Verdict.* Trans. Ewald Osers and Alexandra Dring. New York: Harcourt, 2001.

Finkelstein, Israel, and Neil Asher Silberman. *The Bible Unearthed.* New York: The Free Press, 2001.

Fox, Everett. *Genesis and Exodus: A New English Rendition with Commentary and Notes.* (New York: Schocken, 1983).

Fraser, Sir James Gordon. *New Golden Bough.* Ed. Theodore H. Gaster. New York: Criterion, 1959.

Fredriksen, Paula. *Jesus of Nazareth, King of the Jews.* New York: Vintage, 2000.

Frye, Northrop. *Words with Power.* San Diego: Harcourt, 1990.

Gates, Jr., Henry Louis. *The Signifying Monkey.* New York: Oxford UP, 1988.

Goldhagen, Daniel John. *Hitler's Willing Executioners.* New York: Vintage, 1997.

Grice, Paul. *Part I. Logic and Conversation. Studies in the Way of Words.* Cambridge: Harvard UP, 1989. 1–40.

Grudem, Wayne. "Do Inclusive-Language Bibles Distort Scripture? Yes." *Christianity Today* (Oct. 27, 1997): 26–32.

Hard Sayings of the Bible. Ed. Walter C. Kaiser, Jr., Peter H. Davids, F. F. Bruce, and Manfred T. Brauch. Downers Grove, IL: InterVarsity Press, 1996.

Hare, Robert D. *Without Conscience: The Disturbing World of the Psychopaths Among Us.* New York: Guilford, 1993.

Harper's Bible Dictionary. Gen. Ed. Paul J. Achtenmeier. New York: HarperSanFrancisco, 1985.

Harvey Van A. *The Historian and the Believer: The Morality of Historical Knowledge and Christian Belief.* 1966. Urbana: U of Illinois P, 1996.

Hume, David. *An Enquiry Concerning Human Understanding. An Enquiry Concerning Human Understanding and Other Essays.* Ed. Ernest C. Mossner. New York: Washington Square, 1963. 10–158.

James, William. *Pragmatism. Writings 1902–1910.* New York: Library of America, 1987. 479–624.

Kershaw, Ian. *Hitler: 1889–1936 Hubris.* New York: Norton, 1998.

Kugel, James L. *The Bible as It Was*. Cambridge: Harvard UP, 1997.

Martin, Biddy. "Teaching Literature, Changing Cultures." *PMLA* 112 (1997): 7–25

Matthiessen, F. O. *American Renaissance: Art and Expression in the Age of Emerson and Whitman*. New York: Oxford UP, 1941.

McDannell, Colleen, and Bernhard Lang. *Heaven: A History*. New Haven: Yale UP, 1988.

McKay, David O. *Gospel Ideals: Selections from the Discourses of David O. McKay*. Salt Lake City: Improvement Era, 1953.

Miles, Jack. *Christ*. New York: Knopf, 2001.

—. *God: A Biography*. New York: Knopf, 1995.

Neiman, Susan. *Evil in Modern Thought: An Alternative History of Philosophy*. Princeton: Princeton UP, 2002.

Nietzsche, Friedrich. *Beyond Good and Evil*. *Basic Writings of Nietzsche*. Trans. Walter Kaufmann. New York: Modern Library, 1992. 179–435.

Norris, Kathleen. *The Cloister Walk*. New York: Riverhead, 1997.

Osborne, Grant R.. "Do Inclusive-Language Bibles Distort Scripture? No." *Christianity Today* (Oct. 27, 1997): 33–39.

Pilzer, Paul Zane. *God Wants You to Be Rich: The Theology of Economics*. New York: Simon & Schuster, 1995.

Pojman, Louis P., ed. *Philosophy of Religion*. 2nd ed. Belmont, CA: Wadsworth, 1994.

"Prayer." *Encyclopedia Britannica*. CD Edition. © 1994–2000.

Rensberger, David K. "John: Introduction." *The HarperCollins Study Bible*. Gen Ed. Wayne A. Meeks. New York: HarperCollins, 1993. xvii-xxiv.

Richardson, Robert D., Jr. *Emerson: The Mind on Fire*. Berkeley: U of California P, 1995.

Rosten, Leo, ed. *The Religions of America*. New York: Simon & Schuster, 1975.

Sade, Marquis de. "Dialogue Between a Priest and a Dying Man." *The Marquis de Sade: The Complete Justine, Philosophy in the Bedroom, and Other Writings*. Trans. Richard Seaver and Austin Wainhouse. New York: Grove, 1965. 163–75.

Simon, Stephanie, Nick Anderson, and Tony Perry. "39 in Cult Left Recipes of Death." *Los Angeles Times.* March 28, 1997. A1; A20.
Smith, Joseph. "The King Follett Sermon." *History of the Church.* Vol. 6 of 7 vols. Salt Lake City: Deseret Books, 1980. 302–15.
Starkey, Marion L.. *The Devil in Massachusetts.* 1949. New York: Anchor, 1969.
Stevens, Wallace. *Collected Poetry and Prose.* New York: Library of America, 1997.
Tolstoy, Leo. *Resurrection.* Trans. Rosemary Edmonds. New York: Penguin, 1966.
Tompkins, Jane. "A Short Course in Post-Structuralism." *College English* 50 (1989): 733–47.
Twain, Mark. *Roughing It.* Harper and Brothers Edition. Vol 1. New York: P. F. Collier, n.d.
Weber, Max. *The Protestant Ethic and the Spirit of Capitalism.* 1930. Trans. Talcott Parsons. London and New York: Routledge, 1992.
Whitehead, Alfred North. *Religion in the Making.* 1926. New York: Fordham UP, 1996.
Whitman, Walt. *Poetry and Prose.* New York: Library of America, 1982.
Wilkinson, Bruce. *The Prayer of Jabez.* Sisters, OR: Multnomah, 2000.
Willard, Dallas. *The Divine Conspiracy: Rediscovering Our Hidden Life In God.* New York: HarperSanFrancisco, 1998.
Wilson, A. N. *Jesus: A Life.* New York: Fawcett, 1992.
Wuthnow, Robert. "Pious Materialism: How Americans View Faith and Money." *Christian Century* (Mar. 3, 1993): 238–42.

www.ingramcontent.com/pod-product-compliance
Lightning Source LLC
Chambersburg PA
CBHW030140170426
43199CB00008B/142